A Taste of Australian Food and Wine

A Taste of

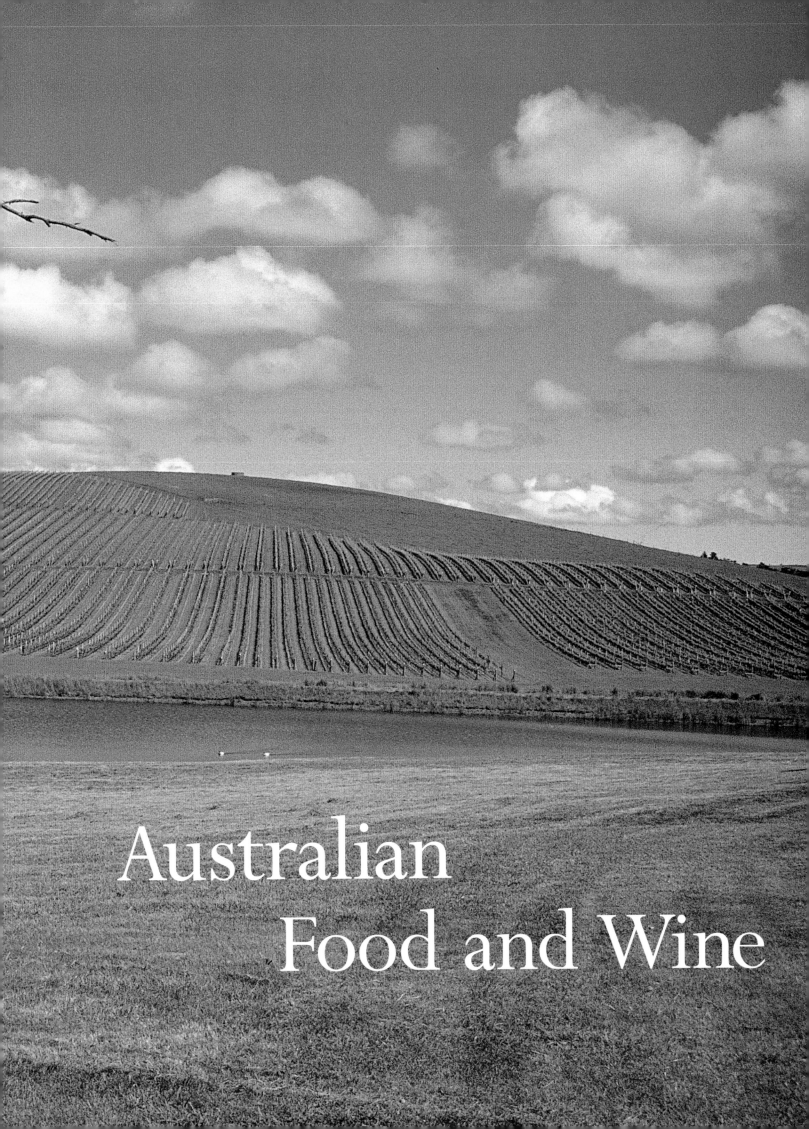

Australian
Food and Wine

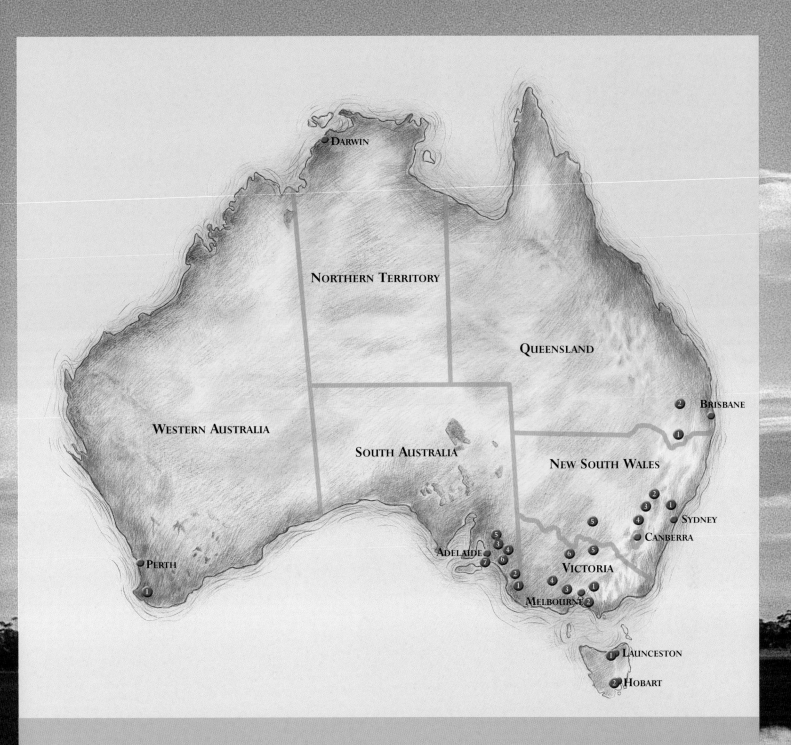

WESTERN AUSTRALIA

1 Margaret River

SOUTH AUSTRALIA

1 Coonawarra
2 Padthaway
3 Barossa Valley
4 Eden Valley
5 Clare Valley
6 Adelaide Hills
7 McLaren Vale

VICTORIA

1 Yarra Valley
2 Mornington Peninsular
3 Macedon Ranges
4 Pyrenees
5 Rutherglen and King Valley
6 Goulburn Valley

QUEENSLAND

1 Mt Tamborine
2 Granite Belt

TASMANIA

1 Northern Tasmania
2 Southern Tasmania

NEW SOUTH WALES

1 Upper and lower Hunter Valley
2 Mudgee
3 Orange
4 Cowra
5 Riverina

Japanese Peppered Beef Sirloin
with Braised Mushrooms
Jackson's Restaurant, Perth.

ACKNOWLEDGEMENTS

First, a big thank you to our photographer, Ian Baker, who has captured through his lens the variety and vibrancy of the Australia culinary and viticultural scene.

For this project we worked closely with Peter Fuller & Associates and we are grateful for their participation in this project. Sally Marden has written the informative and interesting text on the food and wine regions. William Fuller travelled with Ian organising the itinerary and collating the information.

There are many people to thank for helping put this project together. I especially wish to thank Barbara Nielsen for her untiring efforts with co-ordinating the project, Elisabeth Pedersen for her meticulous checking of the recipes and Sally Hollis McLeod for her inspiring design.

Lastly, special thanks to the talented chefs from restaurants and vineyards who so kindly gave their time, their recipes and their wine recommendations for the photography. As this was an independent production, without them we could not have produced this book. We were delighted with the reception and enthusiasm we received and a list of participants is on page 202.

To you all a sincere thank you.

CLIFF JOSEPHS

SPECIAL THANKS TO AGFA-GEVAERT LIMITED, AUSTRALIA, WHO PROVIDED ALL FILM AND PROCESSING.

Introduction

It is seldom that a publisher has the opportunity to develop a concept which fits easily into what the discerning food and wine lover would want in a book. *A Taste of Australian Food and Wine* is such a title. When we discussed the idea with chefs and winemakers the reply from everyone was, 'Yes, we would love to participate. People seldom ask a chef which wine they would match with a dish or ask winemakers what to eat with their wines.'

So we set off on the journey with a flexible itinerary to capture the essence of Australian food and wine. What a magnificent reception we received at wineries and restaurants, where we were privileged to enjoy great hospitality and witness the enthusiasm and energy of the industry.

The chefs provided a selection of the best and freshest produce, including Australia's famous local specialities. You will find recipes using seafood such as yabbies, ocean trout, king prawns, lobster, Tasmanian salmon and Margaret River marron tails; meats such as lamb, beef, veal, kangaroo and pork sausages; local produce such as Barossa verjuice, jarrah-smoked tomatoes and fresh Queensland fruit. Ingredients from Asia, Italy and Greece reflect Australia's cosmopolitan population and the influence of foreign flavours and ingredients on our evolving cuisine.

Good food calls for good wine and you will find excellent examples throughout the book. The wines selected were often personal favourites of the chef or winemaker. You will find something to suit every palate, every dish – refreshing Riesling, spritzy Sauvignon Blanc and rounded, mouthfilling Semillon and Chardonnay in the whites. Or for red wine lovers, there is robust Shiraz or Cabernet Sauvignon, with fine Pinot Noir, juicy Merlot and fascinating blends as well. The breadth of the selection illustrates Australia's current well-deserved position as a leader on the world stage. After recent record harvests, and record exports, there has been huge expansion in vineyard plantings and much development at cellar doors. Regions such as Tasmania, Queensland and Western Australia are now developing as much of a wine tourism ethos as the Hunter Valley, Barossa Valley and the Yarra have long enjoyed.

We would like to have included more restaurants and wineries, but that's another book. The hardest decision was which to select, as there were so many deserving of inclusion.

We wish you as much pleasure in reading and using this book as we had in producing it and hope it will inspire you to explore more of the delights of Australian food and wine.

South Australia

There have been vines cloaking the rolling hills and vales of South Australia since the state was first settled by Europeans in the 1840s. The early pioneers from Germany, England and Eastern Europe were mostly farmers and in this area they found an ideal Mediterranean climate to grow produce, raise livestock and make wines.

With such a heritage, perhaps it's no surprise that here is a largely rural state where people have a refreshingly down-to-earth approach to fine wine and food, and almost take it for granted. Whether in the regions or the towns, shoppers, retailers and restaurateurs simply demand and expect the best wine and freshest, cheapest produce available – because it's what South Australia does.

Adelaide, the attractive, easy-living state capital, is a prime example. It maintains an astonishing selection of restaurants, cafés and bars for its size, as well as the wonderful Central Markets, where the range and extent of food is simply stunning. Here you can find oysters, yabbies, fresh and smoked fish; free-range game birds, duck and poultry; prime beef, venison and lamb; traditional smoked bacon, wursts, pâtés and pies; cow's, sheep and goat's milk cheeses; and every kind of vegetable, fruit, herb and spice imaginable. Authentic cuisine of every type sits side-by-side with the ever-evolving modern Australian food; prices are keen, diners and drinkers are well informed – and extremely well fed.

As if that were not enough, the state also produces perfect wines to go with all this produce. Adelaide might be small compared to many Australian cities, but South Australia is the country's undisputed capital of wine, with 275 producers making almost half the nation's wine, from everyday barbecue quaffers to the finest world-beating reds. It is the state's lifeblood.

The green expanses of vineyard yield every style – intense, full-blooded Shiraz from vines dating back to settlement; steely crisp Riesling and Chardonnay from the cool climate hills; elegant Cabernet, lemony Semillon, luscious stickies and dazzling sparklers. The regions where they are grown and made are just as diverse – pretty valleys, steep-sided hills, gum-studded ranges, coastal plains – as are the foods that are grown and cooked alongside them.

For the serious wine and food lover, the cornucopia that is South Australia is the only place to start.

The Barossa Valley

Botrytis-poached Pears with Yoghurt Cinnamon Bavarois

WITH ROAST QUINCE ICE CREAM AND
MACADAMIA BISCOTTI

Bavarois

150ml pouring cream

2 vanilla pods, split lengthwise

3 cinnamon sticks

3 star anise

100g caster sugar

4 leaves gelatine (or 2 teaspoons powdered)

310g Greek-style set yoghurt

300ml pouring cream

macadamia nut oil for greasing moulds

Poached Pears

8 firm pears

1.5 litres botrytised wine

juice of 1 lemon

200g white sugar

Bavarois: in a saucepan combine 150ml of cream with scraped seeds from vanilla pods, the pods, cinnamon sticks, star anise and sugar. Stir over low heat until sugar has dissolved. Bring to the boil, remove from heat and let stand for 5 minutes. Strain into a large bowl.

Soak gelatine leaves in cold water for about 3 minutes or until soft. Drain and squeeze out excess liquid. Add gelatine to hot cream and stir until completely dissolved. (Or soften powdered gelatine in 2 tablespoons cold water, dissolve in microwave oven for 30–40 seconds. Add to hot cream.) Cool to room temperature.

Whisk yoghurt into the cooled cream mixture. Whip 300ml of cream until soft peaks form. Gently fold into yoghurt mixture.

Lightly grease 8 dariole moulds with macadamia nut oil. Divide the bavarois mixture between the moulds, cover and refrigerate to set.

Poached Pears: peel pears and place in a large, wide saucepan. Add the wine, lemon juice and sugar. Cover and cook over a medium heat for about 30 minutes, or until pears are soft yet still firm in the centre. Test pears with a skewer. Cool in the poaching liquid.

To serve: un-mould a bavarois on to each plate. Place a pear on each plate and drizzle over a little poaching syrup.

The chef has added pear slices, quince ice cream and macadamia biscotti.

Serves 8

Seeing the light at Rymill Coonawarra's stunning cellar door. Completed in 1995, the evocative building houses offices and cellar door sales as well as the state of the art winery. Rymill specialises in Cabernet Sauvignon, Shiraz and Sauvignon Blanc made by senior winemaker John Innes, whose wines reflect the unique Coonawarra terra rossa soil and microclimate.

WINE

Rymill 1997 June Traminer

Sweet wines are a perfect accompaniment to a luscious dessert, enhancing flavours and providing a clean finish.

Tim Foster of The Sweet Grape in Coonawarra's main township, Penola, recommends a glass of Rymill's June Traminer as the ideal complement to his botrytised poached pears.

RECIPE PREPARED BY
TIM FOSTER
THE SWEET GRAPE, PENOLA

Beef Scotch Fillet

IN A MUSTARD MARINADE

4 beef scotch fillet steaks, trimmed
oil for frying

Mustard Marinade
2 tablespoons mild English mustard
2 tablespoons wholeseed mustard
2 tablespoons parsley flakes
1 tablespoon mint flakes
1 tablespoon olive oil
white wine

Mix all marinade ingredients with enough white wine to make a creamy consistency. Marinate meat for at least 2 hours. (This marinade is excellent for lamb fillets also.) Fry steaks in a little hot oil in a heavy-based pan or cook on an oiled hotplate until done to your liking.

Serve steaks with oven-cooked potato wedges and a crisp green salad with yoghurt and garlic dressing.

Serves 4

RECIPE PREPARED BY
PAULA DAHL
NIBS RESTAURANT, COONAWARRA

In 1993 it occurred to winemakers Brian Lynn and Bill Brand that there was nowhere in the Coonawarra they could sneak away to during vintage and enjoy a prime grilled steak and a bottle of their local red in a casual atmosphere. They set about renovating the old schoolhouse and Nibs Restaurant — with its central indoor 'cook your own' barbecue — was born.

Now owned and managed by Paula and Darcy Dahl, Nibs continues to provide the best in prime-grown South-East beef, lamb, chicken and salmon from local aquaculture farms. The restaurant exudes a friendly country atmosphere and most evenings at the barbecue you're bound to rub shoulders with a local winemaker and enjoy a glass of their red.

WINE

Penley Estate 1998 Phoenix Cabernet Sauvignon

A great steak deserves a great red and the 1998 Penley Estate Cabernet Sauvignon is the perfect red meat lover's wine. The Phoenix is a lovely medium-weight yet richly complex red with well-handled oak wrapping itself nicely around spicy Coonawarra fruit. The wine is made by Kym Tolley, part of a famous South Australian winemaking dynasty, who established Penley Estate in 1988.

Coonawarra, the 'Bordeaux of the South'

The essence of Coonawarra's fame is a cigar-shaped strip of limestone, 15 kilometres long and 1.5 kilometres wide, covered by a thin layer of red terra rossa soil. Laid down more than 650,000 years ago, as the seas that covered Australia retreated to the south, the geological structure provides exceptional drainage, along with easy access for vine roots to underground water trapped in the limestone.

This soil structure and the region's cool climate have combined to produce arguably Australia's greatest Cabernet Sauvignon, as well as exceptional Shiraz. The first winery was established in Coonawarra in the late 1800s by philanthropic grazier John Riddoch, who had a vision of a self-sufficient fruit colony. However, it wasn't until the 1960s that the region really took off with such major Australian companies as Wynns, Lindemans, Penfolds and Mildara recognising the unique viticulture conditions and turning it into the 'Bordeaux of the South'.

Lindemans winery buildings sit in attractive, manicured grounds and feature a spacious tasting area.

The Lynn family, owners of Majella, have a fascinating collection of paintings in their cellar door, including the aptly named 'Time to Indulge' by Rozy Reeves.

The Malleea, the 1998 vintage of Majella Wines' Cabernet Sauvignon and Shiraz blend.

Spiced Tatiara Lamb Stack

WITH ROAST VEGETABLES AND NATIVE PEPPER LEAF GLAZE

1.5kg or 6 lamb loin fillets (backstrap fillets)
oil for cooking

Dry Spice Mix for Lamb
1 1/2 tablespoons ground native pepper leaf*
2 teaspoons cracked black pepper
1 tablespoon Maldon sea salt
2 teaspoons onion powder
1 teaspoon ground oregano

Roast Vegetables
4 small potatoes, halved
1 zucchini cut into thick slices
4 roma tomatoes, halved
6 tablespoons olive oil
sea salt

Native Pepper Leaf Sauce
1 1/2 tablespoons butter
1 1/2 tablespoons flour
100ml port
300ml stock
12 whole native pepper leaves*

The Limestone Coast viticultural and winemaking zone is part of a substantial grazing, horticultural and cropping region known as the South-East of South Australia. The region is distinctively flat with towering red gums rising out of vast cattle and sheep grazing paddocks and an increasing spread of premium vineyards.

Lamb: remove silverskin from lamb fillets. Combine all the spices and rub into the lamb. Allow to sit for 12–24 hours. Heat a lightly oiled, heavy-based pan and sear the lamb on all sides. Finish in a moderate oven for 6–7 minutes.

Roast Vegetables: precook the potato halves in boiling water, or microwave for 6 minutes. Coat all vegetables with olive oil and a sprinkling of salt. Roast in a moderate oven for 15 minutes.

Sauce: Melt butter, add flour and mix to a smooth paste (beurre manié). Add the port to the pan used for cooking the lamb and deglaze. Add stock and pepper leaves. Simmer for 5 minutes. While whisking the port/stock mixture constantly, crumble in the flour/butter mixture a little at a time to thicken the sauce. Stop adding the beurre manié when the sauce reaches the desired consistency.

To serve: on each plate make a stack of roast vegetables, starting with potatoes and finishing with a tomato half (cut side uppermost) on top. Add fanned slices of lamb fillet and some sauce.

*For the 12 native pepper leaves you can substitute 1 teaspoon of roasted, cracked white peppercorns, but this will not impart the same floral characters as pepper leaf.

Serves 4–6

WINE

Zema Estate 1998 Coonawarra Cabernet Sauvignon

Zema Estate, established in 1982, makes renowned and distinctive varietal wines including Sauvignon Blanc, Merlot, Malbec, Shiraz, Cabernet Franc and Cabernet Sauvignon. The 1998 Cabernet Sauvignon displays the vibrant fruit flavours and full berry characteristics for which Coonawarra is renowned, and is an ideal match for the Spiced Tatiara Lamb from Chardonnay Lodge.

RECIPE PREPARED BY
CRAIG ZOBRINICH
CHARDONNAY LODGE, COONAWARRA

Smoked Salmon on Fried Corn Cakes

WITH AVOCADO, RED ONION AND CAPERS
AND CRÈME FRAICHE

Corn Cakes
1 cob sweet corn
1/2 small red onion, finely diced
1 tablespoon chopped coriander
1 small clove garlic, peeled, finely chopped
2 teaspoons sweet chilli sauce
1 egg
100ml cream
50g flour
30ml olive oil

12 slices Springs smoked salmon, or salmon
   of your choice
1 large reed avocado
1/2 small red onion, finely diced
20g salted tiny capers
150g crème fraîche or sour cream

Cut kernels from corn cob with a sharp knife.
Mix well with onion, coriander, garlic, chilli
sauce, egg, cream and flour. Let mixture rest
for 15 minutes.

Meanwhile make smoked salmon 'roses' by
folding each slice in half lengthwise and rolling
into a rose shape. Peel and cut avocado into
1cm dice. Mix with onion and rinsed capers.

Place a large, heavy-based frying pan over
moderate heat, add olive oil and spoon in 12
small pancakes. Cook for 2 minutes, turn, then
cook for 2 more minutes. Remove and drain.
Arrange 3 corn cakes on each plate with a
heaped tablespoon of crème fraîche in the
centre. Place avocado mixture in small piles
between the corn cakes. Top each corn cake
with a salmon rose.

Serves 4
as an entrée or light lunch

RECIPE PREPARED BY
SUZY CHANT
THE HERMITAGE CAFÉ AND WINE BAR,
COONAWARRA

Eucalyptus gumnuts stud the Coonawarra landscape.

*In the interests of preserving and maintaining a regional food
culture, salmon from Cape Jaffa on the Limestone Coast is smoked
at Mount Barker in the Adelaide Hills then returns to the region for
Suzy Chant of Coonawarra's Hermitage Restaurant to use for her
smoked salmon roses (opposite). Suzy established the Hermitage ten
years ago and is one of the many restaurateurs in the Coonawarra
who is promoting local and South Australian produce, not only to
support local farmers but also to achieve premium quality.*

WINE

Katnook Estate 1999 Sauvignon Blanc
*Katnook Estate was established in 1980 and now
owns a substantial 240 hectares of vineyard in the
Coonawarra. Their 1999 Sauvignon Blanc, produced
by senior winemaker Wayne Stehbens, is crisp, tangy
and clean as a whistle, a perfect foil for smoked
salmon with corn cakes.*

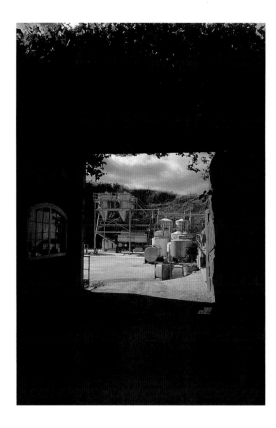

Robert and Geoff Schrapel, fifth generation descendants of the first settlers, create classic examples of all Barossa styles, at Bethany, the Barossa's first settlementt.

The Barossa

The Barossa is home to some of the world's oldest vines, surviving from the 1840s when Silesian Lutherans first put down roots here. It is ancient vines like these and the region's warm, dry climate that makes Barossa Shiraz one of the world's great red wines – rich, ripe, full-bodied and spicy. Grenache, Mourvedre and Cabernet produce reds in similar vein, but winemaking in what is widely regarded as Australia's most important wine region is not confined to reds.

Up in the cooler hills of the Barossa's Eden Valley, steely, lime-scented Riesling is produced, and luscious lemony Semillon thrives throughout.

The lush green rows of vines provide welcome contrast to the acres of dry pasture land surrounding the Barossa in summer months.

The rolling ranges which flank the Barossa Valley provide plenty of superb vantage points and viewing areas of this beautiful region.

Vegetarian Antipasti:

HUMMUS, BABA GHANOUSH, TABBOULEH,
CARROT SALAD, KALAMATA OLIVES AND
TOASTED ZAHTAR BREAD FINGERS
WITH MARINATED MUSHROOMS, ARTICHOKES,
TOFETTA AND TOFU

BABA GHANOUSH

2 large eggplants (aubergines)
1/4 cup plain yoghurt
2 tablespoons lemon juice
1 clove garlic, peeled, crushed
1/4 cup tahini
2 teaspoons ground cumin
1/3 cup fresh coriander

Pierce eggplants in several places with a fork or fine skewer. Bake, whole, uncovered, in a hot oven 200–225°C for 1 hour. Cool for 15 minutes. Peel eggplants then chop. Blend in a food processor with remaining ingredients.
Makes about 2 1/4 cups.

HUMMUS

2 cups dried chick peas (soaked overnight)
2 teaspoons oil
1 medium-sized brown onion, chopped
2 cloves garlic, peeled, crushed
1 teaspoon ground, hot paprika
1 1/2 teaspoons ground cumin
1/4 cup soy milk
1/2 cup tahini
1/2 cup lemon juice
1 tablespoon chopped, fresh coriander

Drain soaked chick peas. Cook in fresh water until tender. Drain, reserving cooking water.
Heat oil and add onion, garlic and paprika. Stir until onion is soft. Add cumin and chick peas and stir until fragrant. Stir in soy milk. Blend in a processor with remaining ingredients, adding enough reserved liquid to make a smooth, thick purée.

CARROT SALAD

Toss finely shredded carrot with some dried currants and a little rosewater.

TOASTED ZAHTAR BREAD FINGERS

Slice focaccia into strips (15cm by 2.5cm), brush with oil and sprinkle with zahtar (a thyme, sumac, salt, sesame seed mixture), then grill.

TABBOULEH

3/4 cup cracked wheat (bulgur)
3/4 cup chopped flat-leaf parsley
3/4 cup chopped mint
6 spring onions, chopped
cherry tomatoes and roasted pine nuts to garnish

Dressing

1/4 cup lemon juice
1/4 cup olive oil
sea salt and freshly ground black pepper
a pinch chilli flakes
1 teaspoon ground cinnamon

Soak wheat in 1 1/2 cups hot water for about 15 minutes. Drain well. Add parsley, mint and spring onions, and mix well. Combine all dressing ingredients and add to the salad. Garnish with halved cherry tomatoes and roasted pine nuts.

To serve Antipasti: arrange together on a platter the Hummus, Baba Ghanoush, Carrot Salad, Tabbouleh, olives, Toasted Zahtar Bread Fingers and salad greens.

The chef has added tofetta (organic tofu blended with olive and safflower oils, herbs and spices) marinated mushrooms and artichokes, and tofu.

RECIPES PREPARED BY
BEV ZILM
ZILM'S GOURMET CAFÉ AT
CRANEFORD WINES

Undulating sheep and wheat farming country between Truro and Nuriootpa gives way to the vineyards of the Barossa.

WINE

Craneford 1999 Quartet

John and Bev Zilm's winery and café sit happily together in the old Truro fire station, tables and tanks side by side.
Their Quartet is a classic European-style blend of Shiraz, Cabernet Sauvignon, Cabernet Franc and Petit Verdot. With a lovely spicy French oak nose, and soft, long, layered palate, it is complex enough to handle any food well.

Roast Duck Breast

WITH ORANGE, BLACK OLIVE AND RED ONION SALAD,
ROCKET AND VERJUICE VINAIGRETTE

6 duck breasts
oil for cooking
salt and pepper

Salad

6 oranges
2 medium-sized red onions, peeled
250g black olives, pitted
1 bunch coriander
1 large bunch rocket

Vinaigrette

2 tablespoons verjuice (or lemon juice)
1 tablespoon lemon juice
4 tablespoons olive oil
sea salt and pepper
good pinch of sugar
2 teaspoons Dijon mustard (or to taste)

Duck: preheat oven to 200°C. Lightly oil a frying pan. Season duck just prior to cooking. Place duck breasts, skin sides down, in the hot pan (do not crowd pan; you may need to sear in batches), and cook until skin is well coloured. Turn and quickly sear the other side.

Finish cooking (skin side up), in a hot oven for 10 minutes for medium-rare (or less for rare, longer for medium). Remove from oven and let rest in a warm place until required.

Salad: cut peel and pith from oranges. Slice oranges into rounds. Place in a bowl with any juice. Cut onions in halves then slice as finely as possible. Combine onions, oranges and olives. Wash and finely chop coriander and stir through the salad. If possible, leave covered at room temperature until required. If refrigerated, bring to room temperature before serving.

Vinaigrette: mix all ingredients well, taste, and adjust seasoning if necessary. Stir most of the vinaigrette into the orange salad, reserving a little for the rocket.

To serve: remove skin from duck then cut across the grain into fine slices. Arrange on top of orange salad. Dress the rocket with vinaigrette and arrange on the duck.

Serves 6

RECIPE PREPARED BY
KAS MARTIN
ST HALLETT'S CAFÉ AND BISTRO

An old vine knots its way around a verandah post at St Hallett Wines in the Barossa. It provides leafy shade over the winery's Café & Bistro, opened in 1999 to give winery visitors a rounded experience of Barossa food and wine. Chef Kas Martin is dedicated to matching her menu with the premium wines that St Hallett has been producing since the historic company was born again in the 1980s. Wines such as Old Block, sourced from 100-year-old Shiraz vines, and Poacher's Blend, a refreshing, lively white blend, keep diners and cellar door guests coming back.

WINE

St Hallett 1999 Gamekeeper's Reserve

Gamekeeper's Reserve, a blend of Grenache, Shiraz, Touriga and Mourvedre, was created by St Hallett winemaker Stuart Blackwell. The 1999 vintage produced brilliant fruity Shiraz and Touriga, Mourvedre with backbone and concentrated Grenache owing to the dryness of the season. The wine shows lifted berry, spicy, gamy and chocolate flavours — ideal to match with roast duck.

Capsicum and Goat Milk Curd Bruschetta

Take an 8cm long French baguette or bread stick and cut in half lengthwise. Brush each piece with olive oil and put in the oven to brown. When brown, spread each piece with goat milk curd cheese. Spread Maggie Beer Products* Vegetarian Capsicum Pâté on top. Drizzle over a dressing of olive oil, red wine vinegar, salt and pepper. Serve with rocket.

*Maggie Beer's Vegetarian Capsicum Pâté is available at good food stores throughout Australia.

RECIPE PREPARED AT
MAGGIE BEER'S PHEASANT FARM SHOP
BAROSSA

WINE

Pheasant Farm 1999 Barossa Semillon

Maggie Beer and husband Colin have turned to Barossa wine as well as food. Their Pheasant Farm Barossa Semillon is made at Yalumba and sold at Maggie's Farm Shop. It is typical of the region's style, with lemon and citrus characteristics on the nose and a luscious, lemony palate.

Chef and food writer Maggie Beer is one of the Barossa's most passionate exponents. In 2000 she opened her Pheasant Farm Shop, a showcase of her own regional gourmet foods, books, local produce and wine, with an airy café attached. Sitting just outside the village of Marananga, between Nuriootpa and Tanunda, the lakeside shop and café is a peaceful spot to enjoy a light lunch and the latest Maggie Beer creations.

Sweet Onion Tart

WITH BAROSSA GOAT MILK CHEESE, ROCKET AND OLIVES

Pastry
  250g plain flour
  pinch of salt
  50g butter
  2 egg yolks
  110ml water
  1 teaspoon lemon juice

Sweet Onion Mixture
  3 medium-sized red onions, sliced
  50ml olive oil
  60g brown sugar
  2–3 pinches ground cloves
  110ml red wine vinegar
  1 bay leaf
  salt and pepper

Dressing
  100ml extra virgin olive oil
  50ml balsamic vinegar
  salt and pepper

For each serving
  80–100g goat milk cheese, 6–8 black olives,
  a bunch of rocket

Pastry: rub flour, salt and butter together to a
sandy texture. Add wet ingredients and mix to
form a dough. Cover and refrigerate for 2
hours. Roll out pastry to 2–3 mm thickness
then let rest for 30 minutes in the fridge. Line
tart tins (10cm diameter, 1cm deep) or your
choice of baking mould, with pastry.
  Bake blind at 170°C until light brown.
Remove bake-blind material, reduce oven to
150°C and bake for 5 more minutes, or until
evenly golden. Remove and cool on a rack.

Onion Mixture: sauté onion in oil until slightly
brown. Add sugar and cook until sugar starts to
caramelise. Add ground cloves, then vinegar
and bay leaf. Cook over medium heat until the
liquid has almost gone. Season. Remove bay leaf.

Dressing: whisk all ingredients together.

To assemble: fill tart shells with onion mixture
and place goat milk cheese on top. Bake at
170°C for 5 minutes. Place olives on a plate
with a tart in the centre. Top with rocket and
drizzle with dressing.

Serves 10

RECIPE PREPARED BY
PETER CLARKE
VINTNERS BAR & GRILL, ANGASTON

*Exotic Barossa Mushrooms with Wild Duck and a Pea Risotto,
above, another delicious dish prepared by Peter Clarke.*

*Vintners Bar & Grill is a favourite haunt of local winemakers,
who know inspired regional cooking and an impressive wine list
when they see them.*

WINE

Mountadam 1997 Pinot Noir

*Mountadam planted Pinot Noir vines in the chilly
upper echelons of the High Eden Ridge back in the
1960s. Burgundy-trained Adam Wynn thought it
was perfect Pinot country; winemaker Andrew Ewart
proves him right with this silky smooth wine showing
sensual raspberry and wild cherry highlights.*

*From barrel to bottle —
Seppelt's stunning Barossa
property is still very much
a working winery as well
as a living historical
monument, with table wines
like these produced and
precious old fortifieds blended
and stored in barrels.*

Seppeltsfield

Seppeltsfield, the Seppelt family winery and the village that grew around it,
is a living wine museum and a true Barossa landmark. Founded by a migrant
Polish chemist in the 1860s, Seppelt was the biggest winery in Australia at the
turn of the 20th century and houses the country's biggest stocks of aged fortified
wines to this day. The pristine historic cellars, winery buildings and gardens are
reached from all directions via long roads lined with date palms, the planting of
which was ordered by the benevolent Seppelt family to keep their workers
employed during the Depression. Seppelt Wines today produces a full range of
wines, with renowned Barossa Cabernet Sauvignon, Eden Valley Riesling and a
raft of sparkling wines made at its Great Western winery in Victoria. But it is
the Seppelt fortified wines that continue to dominate and attract most attention;
they produce some of the finest tawny port and sherry style wines in Australia.

*Ivy-clad windows of the historic
cellar and office complex, which
overlooks some of the famous
Seppelt palm trees.*

Aged Beef Fillet

WITH BAROSSA MUSHROOM RISOTTO,
JARRAH-SMOKED TOMATOES, PARMIGIANO AND
TRUFFLE OIL

Risotto

   5 cups chicken stock

   2 tablespoons butter

   1 onion, chopped

   100g wild mushrooms, sliced*

   2 cups arborio rice

   1 cup beef jus

Beef

   2kg aged beef fillet, trimmed

   cracked black pepper

   sea salt

   extra virgin olive oil

   16–20 jarrah-smoked or semi-dried tomatoes

   1/2 cup shaved Parmigiano or parmesan

   truffle oil to taste

Risotto: bring chicken stock to the boil. Heat butter in a large, heavy-based pan and sauté onion and mushrooms. Add the rice, stirring for 2 minutes to thoroughly coat grains.

Add 1 cup of chicken stock at a time, stirring until liquid has been absorbed before adding more. Cook, stirring until all stock is in. Set aside.

Beef: coat beef fillet with pepper, sea salt and oil. Seal meat in a hot pan, then transfer to a hot oven, about 225°C, for 18 minutes. Let rest in a warm place for 10 minutes.

While beef is resting reheat the risotto and add beef jus. Carve beef into thick slices, each 125–150g.

To serve: place risotto on plates with sliced beef and tomatoes. Top with shaved parmesan. Drizzle with a small amount of truffle oil.

Serves 6

*The pine forests of the Barossa Valley are an amazing source of edible fungi, including Australian ceps, orange caps and field mushrooms. Their flavour, along with South Australian aged beef, is earthy and intense – a fabulous match for Barossa Shiraz.

RECIPE PREPARED BY
VINCE AND WENDY TROTTA
SALTERS RESTAURANT, SALTRAM WINE ESTATES

WINE

Saltram 1998 No 1 Shiraz

The Barossa is most famous for its big Shiraz, and the No 1 Shiraz from Saltram, made by Nigel Dolan, is a classic example. The 1998 is a rich, full-bodied and deep dark red only beginning to show its long-term potential. After 2 years in American and French Oak it's just right to partner this rich, aged-beef fillet recipe.

Wines served at Salters Restaurant, Saltram Wine Estates, just out of Angaston. Vince and Wendy Trotta took over the restaurant in late 2000, bringing to it a popular 'new Australian'-style menu.

Stephen Henschke, winemaker, and his viticulturist wife Prue run the historic family winery and vineyards up in the cool, gum-strewn grazing country of the Eden Valley, where they produce some of Australia's finest table wines.
The Henschkes' 80ha of mature vineyard holding includes the legendary 130-year-old Hill of Grace Shiraz block.

When it was built in 1890, Chateau Tanunda (right) was the biggest building in the Southern Hemisphere and the major employer in the Barossa. These days, this impressive building has a quieter role as a lovingly restored landmark with a stunning new cellar door and function centre.

Barossa-built

Beautiful old buildings and properties dot the Barossa landscape, and most are still in use today. From pug cottages to imposing chateaus built in locally quarried bluestone, architectural gems can be found throughout the region. Some of the oldest and most impressive structures are wineries dating back to the mid-1800s, when the early European settlers realised what a perfect winemaking region they had found.

Australia's oldest family-owned winery, Yalumba has built an enviable worldwide reputation for its range of premium red, white and sparkling wines. The business was founded in 1847 by an English brewer, Samuel Smith, and it continues to be run from the magnificent stone and marble buildings (below) he erected in 1900.

Grilled Clare Valley Yabbies

WITH TOMATO RISOTTO

Tomato Risotto

190ml medium-sweet white wine
  (Skillogalee Late Picked Riesling)
165ml chicken stock
1 tablespoon olive oil
1 medium-sized onion, finely chopped
1 cup risotto rice (carnoli or arborio)
25g butter
1/4 cup freshly grated parmesan
1 cup peeled, seeded, diced tomato
1 tablespoon caster sugar
sea salt and freshly ground black pepper

Grilled Yabbies

36 fresh yabbies (small, fresh-water crayfish)
2 tablespoons olive oil
juice of 1 lemon
2 sprigs fresh thyme, finely chopped
1 clove garlic, peeled, finely chopped
6 sprigs fresh thyme to garnish

Tomato Risotto: heat wine and chicken stock until simmering. Heat oil in a second saucepan and gently fry onion until transparent. Add rice (unwashed), and cook for 2 or 3 minutes, stirring constantly, until the oil is absorbed. Add a ladleful of hot stock mixture to the rice and cook until it is absorbed, stirring frequently. Repeat addition of hot stock, stirring frequently, until all liquid is in and rice is just cooked through, but still quite firm, about 20 minutes. Supplement liquid with hot water if necessary; do not add cold liquid.

When rice is tender, add butter, grated parmesan, tomato, sugar and seasoning. Mix gently. Remove from heat and cover.

Yabbies: cook yabbies in briskly boiling water in a large pan for about 2 minutes. Remove and cool quickly under cold running water. Remove 30 yabbie tails from the shells, leaving 6 in the shell for garnishing.

Mix together olive oil, lemon juice, chopped thyme and garlic. Brush this over the tails and grill for about 1 minute.

For each serving: place a large spoonful of risotto in a warm pasta bowl. Arrange 5 grilled yabby tails on top and garnish with a yabby in the shell and a sprig of thyme. Serve immediately.

Serves 6

Yabbies caught wild from the dams and rivers of the region are hugely popular, as is the locally reared and smoked salmon pictured at right. The recipe for Springs Smoked Salmon with Corn Cakes and Avocado Salsa is overleaf.

RECIPE PREPARED BY
DIANA PALMER
SKILLOGALEE WINERY AND RESTAURANT

WINES

Skillogalee 1996 Chardonnay

This Skillogalee Chardonnay from a small, dry, established vineyard shows buttery fullness and balance with a clean, dry finish, making it a perfect yabbie match.

Skillogalee 2000 Riesling

With the smoked salmon, a classic Clare Riesling such as this is ideal, with its delicate floral nose and a dry, biting finish.

Springs Smoked Salmon

WITH CORN CAKES AND AVOCADO SALSA

9 slices smoked salmon (1 1/2 slices per person)
mizuna leaves, washed
sour cream
chopped chives
salt and pepper

Avocado Salsa
  juice of 1 lime
  1/2 spanish onion, finely diced
  1/2 cup coriander leaves
  pinch of ground coriander
  2 tablespoons mango chutney
  1 teaspoon sambal oelek
  extra virgin olive oil
  3 ripe avocados, peeled, diced

Corn Cakes
  kernels cut from 2 corn cobs
  olive oil
  100g self-raising flour
  250ml buttermilk
  2 eggs, separated
  1 1/2 tablespoons chopped coriander leaves
  1 1/2 tablespoons chopped Italian parsley
  oil for frying

Avocado Salsa: combine lime juice, onion, coriander leaves and ground coriander, mango chutney and sambal oelek. Add about 1 tablespoon of olive oil and gently fold in diced avocado. Season to taste.

Corn Cakes: gently fry corn kernels in a little oil. Mix together flour, salt, pepper, buttermilk, egg yolks and herbs. Add corn. Whisk egg whites to soft peak stage and fold through the corn mixture. Heat oil in a frying pan and drop in spoonfuls of mixture. Cook until golden, for about 1 minute each side. Remove and keep warm while the rest are cooked.

To assemble: in the centre of each main course plate stack the following: a corn cake, a few mizuna leaves on top then a spoonful of salsa. Twist a slice of smoked salmon and place on the salsa. Repeat layers once more, finishing with a half slice of salmon. Mix chopped chives with sour cream and place 3 small spoonfuls around the salmon and salsa stack. Serve immediately.

Serves 6 (entrées)

RECIPE PREPARED BY
DIANA PALMER
SKILLOGALEE WINERY AND RESTAURANT

Leasingham was originally an offshoot of the Stanley Wine Co, launching award-winning wines in the sixties. Since 1988, it has thrived under the ownership of BRL Hardy, making benchmark Riesling and structured reds.

Clare Valley

The Clare Valley is one of Australia's prettiest wine regions, with wooded hills and vales and many enticing cellar doors. Wineries vary in size from the boutique to the corporate. Two prime examples are Sevenhill, run by an order of Jesuits, and Leasingham, part of a nationwide network of wineries owned by industry giant BRL Hardy.

Riesling is the star variety here, producing floral-scented, citrus-flavoured whites with hints of perfume and spice that are capable of great ageing. Reds are also good, especially well-structured Shiraz and Cabernet Sauvignon.

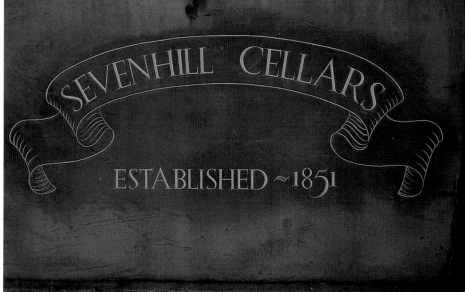

The Sevenhill property was purchased in 1851 by the Society of Jesus. A year later, they planted vines and today the Jesuit winemakers continue to make fine wines on the same site.

Pan-fried Pork Fillet

WITH STEAMED, GINGERED BABY BOK CHOY,
SWEET POTATO CHIPS AND CHILLI PLUM JUS

Chilli Plum Jus
  500ml veal or beef stock
  6 satsuma plums
  2 tablespoons soy sauce
  1 red chilli
  1 tablespoon sugar

  500g pork fillet
  salt and pepper
  oil for frying
  1 sweet potato (kumara)
  8 baby bok choy
  2.5cm piece of fresh ginger, finely chopped
  coriander leaves to garnish

Chilli Plum Jus: poach plums in stock until tender.
Remove plum stones and sieve the mixture into
a pan, pushing the plum flesh through. Add soy
sauce and finely chopped chilli (seeds included if
a hotter sauce is required). Add sugar and simmer to reduce until the liquid coats the back of
a spoon.

Pork: trim the fillet, removing silverskin, then
cut into medallions, allowing 3–4 rounds per
person. Season with salt and pepper. Pan-fry in
a little oil over medium heat until medallions
are golden brown on both sides, and cooked
through. (Using medium heat only will ensure
the meat does not cook too quickly and become
tough.)

Sweet Potato Chips: peel and thinly slice sweet
potato. Deep-fry until golden; drain on
absorbent paper and sprinkle with salt.

Bok Choy: wash and halve bok choy lengthwise.
Mix with ginger and season with salt and pepper.
Steam until just cooked, retaining deep green
colour.

To serve: arrange bok choy on hot plates, top
with pork medallions and add sweet potato
chips and Chilli Plum Jus. Garnish with fresh
coriander leaves.

Serves 4

RECIPE PREPARED BY
PHILIP SCARLES
ELDREDGE VINEYARDS, CLARE VALLEY

*The tranquil view across the garden at Eldredge Vineyards in the
Clare Valley. The restaurant at Eldredge, which overlooks a wild
duck lake, is run by Amanda and Philip Scarles, who specialise
in modern Australian cuisine with a local influence.*

WINE

Eldredge 1999 New Age Grenache
*Leigh Eldredge is senior winemaker at
Eldredge Wines and has been making wines
under this label since 1992. His 1999 Grenache
shows a quite floral nose with soft fruit nuances
and yet is more earthy on the palate, giving
it the texture for food and making it a
good pairing with the pork.*

Zortxiko di Mar

(A BASQUE SEAFOOD DISH)

For each serving
  extra virgin olive oil
  1 teaspoon crushed garlic
  4 fresh greenshell mussels
  6 prawns, shelled
  2 small fillets of white fish (whiting is ideal)
  4 scallops
  1/4 teaspoon chopped chilli
  1/2 cup crushed, fresh tomato
  1/2 cup cream
  salt and pepper to taste

Heat olive oil and garlic in a pan until the pan is very hot. Add mussels in the half-shell (not pre-steamed), prawns and white fish and cook quickly. Add shelled scallops.

In a separate pan heat a dash of olive oil and add chilli, tomato and cream and simmer to reduce the sauce a little. Season to taste.

Arrange seafood on a plate and pour the sauce over the top. Garnish with sprigs of fresh rosemary. Serve with arborio rice and a green salad.

Serves 1

RECIPE PREPARED BY
ANDRÉ VAN DER VEKEN
REILLY'S WINES AND RESTAURANT

WINE

Reilly's 1999 Watervale Riesling
There's nothing quite like a fine dry Riesling to go with seafood and this Watervale wine from Justin Ardill is ideal. It shows all the typical characteristics of a Clare Valley Riesling, with a light floral nose, citrus lime fruit on the palate and tight, dry finish.

Reilly's Winery and Restaurant, originally built in 1856, has been beautifully restored and features an art gallery for regional artists.

Corn-fed Chicken

WITH VEGETABLE VELOUTÉ

4 corn-fed chicken breasts

a little milk

salt, pepper and sugar for seasoning

100g redcurrants

2 medium-sized kumara (sweet potatoes)

16 green asparagus spears

50g butter

200ml vegetable velouté (recipe below)

1 bunch of chives

100ml cream

2 tablespoons Italian white truffle oil

Vegetable Velouté

40g butter

20g (2 tablespoons) flour

250ml vegetable stock

1/2 onion, 1 bay leaf and 2 whole cloves

salt and pepper

Chicken: cut a pocket in each chicken breast and remove the small fillet underneath.

Blend the small fillets in a processor, adding sufficient milk to make a farce (forcemeat mixture should be finely minced and moist). Season with salt and pepper and mix in redcurrants. Use a piping bag to fill the farce into the pockets in chicken breasts. Keep refrigerated until required.

Vegetable Velouté: melt butter in a saucepan, add flour and whisk until smooth. Whisk in stock and let simmer. Add onion studded with bay leaf and cloves. Boil to reduce to a thicker consistency. Remove onion, bay leaf and cloves.

Peel and slice kumara. Boil in salted water until tender, then mash. Add salt and pepper to taste and keep warm.

Poach chicken breasts in water for 10 minutes.

Braise the cleaned asparagus in the butter with salt, sugar and a little water until just cooked.

Reheat velouté and add very finely cut chives. Add salt and pepper to taste. Add cream and mix with a hand blender until frothy.

To serve: place an egg ring on each plate and fill with kumara mash. Remove ring. Arrange asparagus in a square around the mash. Place cooked chicken breast on top. Add frothy sauce to plates. Brush chicken with truffle oil. Serve immediately.

The typical Clare Valley scene has undulating hills, dipping creek beds and towering blue gums.

The country house with its garden full of native and exotic flowers, above, is in Auburn.

Serves 4

RECIPE PREPARED BY
MARTIN HERRMANN
TATEHAMS RESTAURANT & GUESTHOUSE

WINE

Pikes 2000 Sauvignon Blanc Semillon
Winemaker Neil Pike's Sauvignon Blanc Semillon is a great match for Martin Herrmann's recipe. The wine is light, with distinctive aromas of tropical fruit, mineral hints and a touch of herbaceous, green pepper grassiness so typical of Sauvignon, all of which combine to complement the chicken.

Adelaide, hedonist's heaven

Adelaide might be a state capital, but it feels, lives and acts like a wine town. Wine touches most people's lives here in some way, whether they make it, market it, sell it or simply drink it. Everyone knows their stuff, from taxi drivers to teachers, and with the city's wealth of wine bars, cafés and restaurants there are plenty of opportunities to enjoy and learn more.

Adelaide's Glenelg beach.

A dynamic mirror-glass sculpture in the Adelaide Botanic Gardens.

Adelaide is a small city; you're never far from the vast expanses of clear blue sky in country South Australia.

Char-grilled Quail

WITH CRISPY RICE CAKE AND EGGPLANT RELISH

10 quail, halved
fresh coriander sprigs to garnish

Marinade
1–5 cloves garlic, peeled, finely chopped
1 thumb-sized piece ginger, finely chopped
2 tablespoons medium-sweet soy sauce
3 tablespoons light soy sauce
a pinch of five spice powder
1/3 cup dry sherry
1/3 cup peanut oil
1/4 cup water

Rice Cakes
2 cups sushi rice
2 cups water
1 1/2 cups coconut milk
2.5cm piece lemon grass
2.5cm piece ginger, bruised
2 teaspoons soy sauce
oil for deep-frying

Eggplant Relish
4 red onions, cut in medium dice
2 thumb-size pieces ginger, finely diced
5 cloves garlic, peeled, chopped
4 tablespoons olive oil
5–8 red capsicums, seeded, cut in medium dice
about 3 tablespoons fish sauce
350ml rice wine vinegar
3 cups sugar
5 large eggplants, cut in large dice, lightly salted
3 bunches coriander, chopped
1/2 bunch mint, chopped

Quail: combine marinade ingredients. Optional: bone the quail. Marinate quail halves for 24 hours.

Rice Cakes: Cook rice by absorption method with all ingredients except oil. Cool, remove lemongrass and ginger. Form rice into cakes, then deep-fry.

Eggplant Relish: fry onions, ginger and garlic in oil until onion is transparent. Add capsicums, fry a little, then add fish sauce, vinegar and sugar. Cook until thick and almost caramelised.
Fry eggplant, cool, then fold into the onion mixture. Add chopped coriander and mint. Serve warm or cool.

RECIPE PREPARED BY
SCOTT KUERSCHNER, ALI SEEDSMAN, ADAM PALMER
UNIVERSAL WINE BAR, ADELAIDE

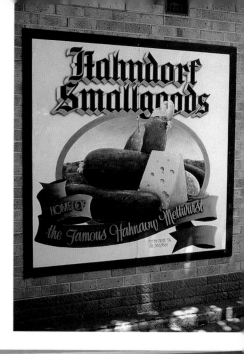

Mettwurst and other speciality smoked meats and sausages have been a feature of Adelaide, the Barossa and the Adelaide Hills since German settlers arrived in the 1840s. These old signs are from Hahndorf, a popular tourist town in the hills west of Adelaide.

Remove quail from marinade and char-grill or barbecue, skin side down, for 5 minutes. Turn and cook for 5 more minutes (3–4 minutes for boned quail).

To serve: arrange a rice cake on each plate with eggplant relish and quail. Garnish with coriander leaves.

Serves 5

WINE

Shaw & Smith 1999 Incognito Merlot
Incognito is the name under which Martin Shaw and Michael Hill-Smith's first red release travels, but there's nothing anonymous about the wine. Luscious red berry fruits and a smooth, soft palate finish with just the right amount of acidity to sit brilliantly with the Universal Wine Bar's Char-grilled Quail.

Veal Rump

WITH PRAWNS, ASPARAGUS AND TRUFFLE CREAM

4 baby veal rumps, each about 200g
8 large prawn tails
12 asparagus spears
100ml white wine
200ml reduced veal stock or light beef stock
1 teaspoon finely chopped truffle
   (or truffle oil, or good, dried mushrooms)
butter
salt and pepper
4 portions of potato or parsnip mash
cream

Trim rumps of sinew and excess gristle. Devein prawn tails. Trim and peel asparagus and cut into 3cm lengths.

Sauce: place wine in a saucepan and simmer to reduce. Add stock and reduce to 150ml. Add minced truffle (or alternative) and stand to infuse.

Veal: pan-fry veal in a little butter. Season with salt and pepper. Place veal in a hot oven (200–225°C) and cook to medium – 10–15 minutes. Set aside and keep warm.

Pan-fry prawns and asparagus in butter for 1 minute.

To serve: place a portion of mash on each plate. Slice veal and stack on the mash with prawns and asparagus. Bring stock to the boil and finish with a little cream and a knob of butter. Serve sauce over veal or around the plate.

Chef's note: a spoonful of Hollandaise sauce complements this dish.

Serves 4

RECIPE PREPARED BY
ALAN WEISS
CHLOE'S RESTAURANT, ADELAIDE

WINE

Henschke 1997 Lenswood Giles Vineyard Pinot Noir

Not the easiest of wine matches this, and yet the Pinot made by Stephen Henschke from Adelaide Hills fruit works well.

The wine shows plenty of characteristic sweet berry fruit, but also has a hint of chocolate and plenty of green spice character. Fine acidity cuts through any richness.

South Australia might be the nation's wine state, but even the winemakers don't like to go too long without a cold beer in one of the many historic and colourful local hotels, whether in the city or in a more remote spot like Marrabel.

Salt and Pepper Lamb Brains

WITH YELLOW THAI DRESSING

6 lamb brains, halved

Poaching Liquor
  1 carrot, 2 stalks celery, cut into small pieces
  1 teaspoon peppercorns
  3 bay leaves
  2.5 litres water
  200ml champagne vinegar

Egg Wash
  500ml milk beaten with 3 eggs

Salt and Pepper Mix
  475g cornflour
  95g (5 tablespoons) salt
  55g (5 tablespoons) ground white pepper
  55g (5 tablespoons) ground black pepper

Spicy Risotto Cakes
  1/2 onion, peeled
  2 cloves garlic, peeled
  100g fresh ginger
  1 tablespoon oil
  2 tablespoons tom yum paste
  2 tablespoons chilli soy paste
  500g risotto rice
  2 litres hot chicken stock
  100ml fish sauce
  oil for deep-frying

Yellow Thai Dressing
  100ml vegetable oil
  100ml sesame oil
  2 onions, diced
  2 stalks lemon grass, chopped
  200g grated ginger
  200g puréed garlic
  1 tablespoon ground turmeric
  1 tablespoon five spice powder
  3 tablespoons red curry paste
  10 fresh kaffir lime leaves
  2 tablespoons soy chilli paste
  125g duck paste*
  250g tom yum paste
  100ml rice wine
  100ml fish sauce
  2.5 litres coconut milk
  100ml oyster sauce
  100ml hoisin sauce

Garnish
  200g Wakame sesame seaweed salad**

WINE
Nepenthe 2000 Sauvignon Blanc
Cool climate Sauvignon from high in the
Adelaide Hills around Adelaide, and showing the
ripe, intense fruit characters for which Nepenthe
has quickly become known. Bright, fresh and tangy,
it smells and tastes of tropical fruit and
finishes sharp and clean.

Brains: combine poaching liquor ingredients in a large saucepan and boil for 10 minutes. Add lamb brains and poach for 3 1/2 minutes. Remove from liquid and refresh in iced water. Drain, and place on an absorbent cloth.

Salt and Pepper Mix: combine all ingredients.

Spicy Risotto Cakes: process (or finely chop) onion, garlic and ginger to a fine paste then fry in oil until golden brown. Add tom yum paste, chilli paste and rice. Cook for 2 minutes, stirring constantly. Add hot stock. Keep stirring on high heat until the stock has been absorbed and the rice is tender. Add fish sauce. Spread out with a spatula in a lined tray. Set in the refrigerator for 3 hours. Cut into 4 circles, each 7cm diameter, or into desired shapes.

Yellow Thai Dressing: heat vegetable and sesame oils in a large pan. Add onion, lemon grass, ginger and garlic. Sauté for 5 minutes. Add remaining ingredients except coconut milk, oyster and hoisin sauces. Sauté for 20 minutes. Stir in coconut milk and bring to the boil. Simmer for 30 minutes. Finally add oyster and hoisin sauces.

To assemble: dip lamb brains in egg wash then coat with salt and pepper mix. Deep-fry until golden brown. Drain and set aside. Deep-fry risotto cakes, drain and set aside. Heat the dressing.

To serve: place a risotto cake on each plate. Arrange 3 lamb lobes on top, garnish with Wakame sesame seaweed salad and add Yellow Thai Dressing.

Serves 4

*Duck paste is an instant soup concentrate. The paste and Wakame sesame seaweed salad **are available at reputable Asian grocery stores.

RECIPE PREPARED BY
TODD LANGLEY
THE OXFORD DINING ROOM
AT THE OXFORD HOTEL

North Adelaide's Oxford Hotel is a hotspot for drinking and dining, particularly since Anthony Parmenter and Jo Albers took over in late 1999 and introduced their take on modern Australian cuisine and wine.

Kangaroo Island
Rock Lobster

BRAISED IN RIESLING · CREAM WITH
POACHED BABY FENNEL

WINE

Penfolds 2000 Eden Valley Reserve Riesling

A classic Eden Valley Riesling made by Penfolds at its Barossa Valley winery, this has floral, rose petal aromas with intensive citrus lime fruit flavours. It could have been made for Chris Matuhina's Rock Lobster in Riesling Cream.

2 small baby fennel bulbs, trimmed
salt
1 live lobster, about 750–800g
150ml cream
100ml Riesling
2 tablespoons chopped chives
1 tablespoon cold butter, diced

Poach the fennel in salted water until tender. Drain and reserve.

Drown the lobster in fresh water, or use a knife to pierce the skull, killing it instantly. Plunge lobster into boiling, unsalted water for about 5 minutes. Refresh in iced water for 5 minutes only (any longer and the flesh will become waterlogged). Drain.

Split the lobster in half and remove flesh, keeping the shells and head for garnish later. Chop flesh into 3cm pieces and reserve.

Simmer the cream and wine until reduced by half. Cut fennel into pieces and add to the cream to warm through. Remove fennel and divide between 2 shallow bowls.

Add lobster pieces to the cream and cook gently for 2–3 minutes; by then the lobster should be cooked through.

Drop the trimmed lobster shell and head into boiling water for 20 seconds to warm up. Place part of the tail next to the fennel.

Remove lobster meat from cream and place on top of the fennel.

Add chives and butter to remaining cream then spoon around the lobster meat. Top with a trimmed piece of the head for garnish if you like. Here the chef has garnished the dish with Springs salmon roe (from Mt. Barker) and fine strands of nori.

Serves 2

RECIPES PREPARED BY
CHRIS MATUHINA
MAGILL ESTATE RESTAURANT, ADELAIDE

Set in the Adelaide foothills, the Magill Estate winery offers fantastic views of Adelaide's skyline, but most diners prefer to concentrate on the stellar food in front of them. Magill Estate is owned by Penfolds, so it comes as no surprise to learn that the wine list is superlative and includes a matchless selection of Grange.

The winery complex is a wonderful blend of original stone buildings and stylish contemporary architecture.

Prawn and Basil Curry

2 tablespoons good vegetable oil

4 lime leaves

2 stalks lemongrass, chopped

2 medium-sized onions, chopped

1 teaspoon fresh ginger and garlic paste*

2 medium-sized tomatoes, chopped

1/2 teaspoon chilli powder

1 teaspoon ground coriander

1 teaspoon ground turmeric

salt to taste

800–850ml (2 cans) coconut milk

600g large green prawns

1 small bunch fresh basil

Heat oil in a pan and add lime leaves, lemongrass and chopped onion. Sauté for a few minutes. Add ginger and garlic paste, chopped tomatoes, chilli powder, coriander, turmeric and salt. Stir well and add coconut milk. Bring to the boil, add prawns and cook for 1 minute. Add torn basil leaves.

Serve hot with naan bread and steamed saffron rice.

*This paste consists of fresh ginger and garlic crushed and blended with oil.

Serves 4

RECIPE PREPARED BY
HEMANT GUSAIN
SIEMERS INDIAN RESTAURANT
ADELAIDE HILLS

WINE

Malcolm Creek 1997 Chardonnay
This wine is made by Reg Tolley, another branch of the Tolley winemaking dynasty, in the Adelaide Hills near Kersbrook. It is a Chardonnay in the classic mould, with fine oak and ripe fruit held in elegant balance, and is well-bred enough to hold its own with this and other curries without being overpowering.

Siemers enticed high profile chef Hemant Gusain from Adelaide's premier Indian restaurant to recreate his range of curries near Stirling in the Adelaide Hills. Here, Prawn and Basil Curry is joined by Rogan Josh, Butter Chicken and Naan bread.

Native trees and plants cloak the Adelaide Hills, providing a taste of the bush for city-dwellers.

Italian Pork Sausages

WITH AMADEUS DEMI-GLAZE, FRIED POLENTA,
GOAT CURD CHEESE AND ROASTED RED CAPSICUM

For each serving

1 teaspoon olive oil

2 fresh Italian all-pork sausages

100ml Cabernet wine

2 wedges homemade polenta (cooled, set)

1 tablespoon goat curd cheese

4–6 strips roasted, peeled capsicum dressed
    with virgin olive oil, crushed garlic,
    chopped parsley, salt and pepper

rosemary sprigs to garnish

Heat the olive oil and add sausages (do not prick them). Cook on medium-to-high heat, turning sausages constantly, for about 7 to 8 minutes. Add red wine, a little at a time, and continue to turn sausages until they are well coated and the wine is almost caramelised.

Pan-fry polenta wedges until golden brown. Arrange polenta wedges on a plate and place a sausage on each. Drizzle remaining pan juices over the sausages. Place chilled curd cheese on the plate. Arrange dressed capsicum slices on the curd. Garnish with rosemary.

Serves 1

Caj & Giannina (Genny) Amadio's Chain of Ponds winery was the pioneer of the Adelaide Hills sub-region of Gumeracha in 1985. As well as making excellent wines, they serve delicious Italian peasant-style food.

WINE

*Chain of Ponds 1998 Amadeus
Cabernet Sauvignon*

This wine complements Genny's cooking to a T, with the pungent bouquet of blackcurrant and cassis, intense flavours and soft lingering finish, standing up perfectly to the robust Italian flavours.

RECIPES PREPARED BY
GENNY AMADIO
CHAIN OF PONDS
ADELAIDE HILLS

Lamb Accatasta

PAN-FRIED LAMB FILLETS WITH GRILLED EGGPLANT
AND PESTO, BABY SPINACH,
ROASTED RED CAPSICUM AND AIOLI

For each serving

baby spinach leaves

olive oil and balsamic vinegar dressing

2 eggplant slices

basil and pine nut pesto

3 small lamb fillets

flour

1 dessertspoon butter

1 clove garlic, peeled, crushed

salt and cracked pepper

lemon juice (optional)

3–4 strips roasted red capsicum dressed with
    olive oil, fresh, crushed garlic,
    chopped parsley, salt and pepper

aioli (garlic mayonnaise)

fresh chopped chillies in olive oil and garlic

Arrange baby spinach leaves on a serving plate, forming a daisy pattern. Drizzle with olive oil/balsamic vinegar dressing.

Grill eggplant slices. Cut them to the same size as the lamb fillets. Baste with pesto and leave aside.

Trim any silverskin from lamb fillets. Butterfly and flatten fillets and flour lightly on both sides.

Heat a non-stick pan and add butter and garlic. Sear lamb fillets, keeping heat medium-to-high. Turn lamb constantly. Work quickly – they take only 2–3 minutes to cook. Add salt and cracked pepper (don't overdo pepper). Drizzle on lemon juice if you like.

Place one lamb fillet on prepared plate of spinach, followed by a layer of eggplant. Repeat layers, finishing with the third fillet on top. Arrange strips of roasted, dressed capsicum on top of lamb. Add a generous spoonful of aioli and serve immediately.

Serve freshly cut hot chillies, dressed in olive oil and garlic, in a separate bowl.

Serves 1

Botrytis Olive Oil Cake

SERVED WITH POACHED PEARS AND TOFFEE GLAZE

Cake

8 egg whites
1/4 teaspoon cream of tartar
3/4 cup sugar
5 egg yolks
1 tablespoon finely grated tangelo or orange rind
1 tablespoon finely chopped almonds
1/3 cup olive oil
1/2 cup botrytised wine (or other sweet dessert wine)
1 cup sifted flour
pinch of salt
icing sugar for dusting cake

Poached Pears with Toffee Glaze

10 whole pears with stems (small beurre bosc)
500ml each white wine and botrytised wine
300g sugar
pinch of saffron filaments
1 cinnamon stick
1/2 tangelo, sliced
2 cups sugar
1 cup water
1/2 tangelo, finely sliced
1 cup of poaching liquid from pears

Cake: grease and line a 23cm springform tin. Beat egg whites, cream of tartar and 1/2 cup of the sugar to soft peak stage. Beat yolks and 1/4 cup of sugar until creamy. Fold together all cake ingredients except icing sugar. Bake at 180°C for 15 minutes, then at 150°C for 20 more minutes. Cool on a wire rack. Dust with icing sugar when cold.

Pears: poach pears (skins on) in the wines with 300g of sugar, the saffron, cinnamon and slices of tangelo, until tender.
Boil together the remaining sugar, water and sliced tangelo until the desired toffee colour is reached. Immediately remove from heat and carefully add 1 cup of poaching liquid.

To serve: cut the cake into wedges. Place a piece of cake on a plate with a whole pear and drizzle with the glaze. Add a dollop of King Island cream if you like. The chef has added poached pear slices and toffee shards to garnish.

Cake serves 8–10

WINES

Woodstock 2000 Verdelho

The ripe, slightly exotic flavours and fine acidity of Woodstock's Verdelho marry well with the light spices in Kay Cazzolato's Smoked Chicken Stack.

Woodstock 1998 Botrytis Sweet White

The combination of Botrytis Olive Oil cake and the deliciously lush Sweet White dessert wine absolutely sing.

RECIPES PREPARED BY
KAY CAZZOLATO
WOODSTOCK WINERY & COTERIE

Smoked Chicken Stack

WITH WONTONS, ROCKET, ASPARAGUS AND AVOCADO, DRESSED WITH CURRY VINAIGRETTE

1 smoked chicken, skinned, boned, sliced
1 bunch rocket
1 avocado, peeled, sliced
2 bunches asparagus, blanched

Wontons

250g flour, sifted
1/2 teaspoon salt
1 egg, lightly beaten
4 tablespoons cold water
brown mustard seeds
coriander leaves
oil for deep-frying

Curry Vinaigrette

2 cups orange juice
1 cup vinegar
1 cup white wine
1 dessertspoon prepared curry paste
1 tablespoon olive oil

Green Vinaigrette

1/2 bunch coriander
1/2 bunch watercress
1 clove garlic, peeled
2 tablespoons vinegar
1/2 cup olive oil

Wontons: combine flour and salt with beaten egg and water. Knead to a smooth dough. Pass the dough through a pasta machine and after the second rolling sprinkle dough with mustard seeds and coriander leaves. Fold, and continue rolling, decreasing thickness to finest setting. Cut to required shape and size. Deep-fry.

Curry Vinaigrette: boil orange juice, vinegar and wine to reduce to 1 cup of liquid. Blend in curry paste and oil. Cool.

Green Vinaigrette: remove coarse stalks from coriander and watercress. In a processor, blend coriander, watercress, garlic and vinegar, adding oil last.

To serve: arrange layers of sliced chicken, rocket, wontons, avocado and asparagus on plates. Dress with curry vinaigrette and drizzle green vinaigrette around for contrast.

Serves 8

Rare-roasted Venison Rump

SERVED ON SPRING ONION AND BACON ROSTI
WITH LEMON THYME, RUM AND
CHOCOLATE GLAZE

4 venison rump steaks, each 180–200g

Rosti

500g potatoes
4 spring onions, trimmed, chopped
10 pepperleaves, finely sliced,
    (or freshly ground black pepper)
100g bacon, finely chopped
salt and pepper
oil for cooking

Glaze

100ml Cabernet Sauvignon wine
50ml port
50ml Bundaberg rum
1 tablespoon chopped lemon thyme
1 tablespoon sugar
500ml beef glaze
50g bitter chocolate
salt and pepper

Olive Paste

20 kalamata olives, pitted
10 capers
3 tablespoons olive oil
black pepper
3 tablespoons chopped parsley

The wooded hillsides of McLaren Vale provide sweeping views of this scenic wine region south of Adelaide.

Venison: tie venison steaks with cooking twine to hold shape while cooking. Seal steaks on a hot, oiled grill-plate then finish in the oven at 180°C to cook to your liking. Allow to rest in a warm place.

Rosti: peel and grate potatoes. Combine with other ingredients except cooking oil. Using plenty of oil, cook the mixture in egg rings (to form neat, round shapes) on the grill-plate until golden on each side. Place on a baking tray and finish cooking in the oven for 10 minutes.

Glaze: simmer wine, port and rum to reduce by half. Add thyme, sugar and beef glaze. Bring to the boil then simmer for 20 minutes. Add chocolate and cook on low heat for another 20 minutes. Adjust seasoning.

Olive Paste: purée all ingredients to a fine paste.

To serve: heat rosti on the grill-plate, reheat venison steaks and reheat glaze. Place rosti in the centre of each plate. Arrange sliced steak on top. Pour the glaze around and garnish with olive paste on top.

Serves 4

RECIPE PREPARED BY
ROGER GRAHAM
LIMEBURNER'S RESTAURANT
MARIENBERG WINES

WINE

Marienburg Reserve Cabernet Sauvignon
Made by Barossa stalwart Grant Burge with McLaren Vale grapes, this wine typifies the region's full-bodied Cabernet style. Herbaceous and leafy on the nose, it tastes soft and fleshy with hints of chocolate and mint.
Roger Graham's roast venison with a lemon thyme, rum and chocolate glaze is a good match.

Baked South Australian Snapper

WITH HALOUMI, ROASTED TOMATO, KALAMATA OLIVES
AND SWEET, AGED VINEGAR DRESSING

6 medium-sized tomatoes

Maldon sea salt

cracked pepper

100ml olive oil
    (McLaren Vale Regional Produce*)

200g haloumi cheese
    (Island Pure, Kangaroo Island*)

50g plain flour

1kg snapper fillet, cut into 8 pieces

120g kalamata olives

3 tablespoons sweet, aged vinegar (Coriole*),
    or balsamic vinegar

80g baby spinach leaves

*Chef's preference.

Halve tomatoes and sprinkle with a little salt
and pepper. Drizzle over some olive oil. Roast
in a low oven, about 160°C, for 2 hours.
(These will keep in the fridge for 2 days so
they can be done ahead.)

Cut haloumi into 8 strips and dust with flour.
Sear in a little oil in a hot pan until golden on
both sides.

Sear fish fillets in remaining olive oil in a large
pan, then place a strip of haloumi on each fillet.
Add tomatoes, olives, salt and pepper and bake
in the oven at 210°C for 14 minutes. Remove
from the oven and add the aged vinegar.

To serve: on each plate arrange 2 snapper fillets
with 2 strips of haloumi, 3 tomato halves and
some baby spinach leaves. Add olives, and pour
over the dressing of pan juices.

Serves 4

RECIPE PREPARED BY
JUSTIN HARMAN
MARKET 190, McLAREN VALE

*One of the many magnificent gum trees that
dot the McLaren Vale hills.*

WINE

Wirra Wirra 2000 Scrubby Rise
*Ben Riggs' blend of Semillon, Sauvignon Blanc and
Chardonnay is a fine balance of fruit complexity,
elegance and structure. It is full-bodied, but has
sufficient acidity to cope with the olives, haloumi
and oil in Justin Harman's baked snapper dish.*

RECIPES PREPARED BY
PETER HOGG
SALOPIAN INN

Goose Egg Tart

WITH FRESH ASPARAGUS, SHAVED PECORINO CHEESE
AND OLIVE OIL AND SHERRY VINEGAR DRESSING

Base
175g plain flour
a pinch of paprika
a pinch of salt
1½ tablespoons grated parmesan
150g cold, unsalted butter, cubed
100g fresh goat milk cheese
1 egg yolk

Goose Egg Mixture
1 medium-sized onion, peeled
2 goose (or 6 hen or duck) eggs, hard-boiled
salt and pepper
1 bunch chives, finely chopped
250–300ml homemade mayonnaise

Garnish
12–24 asparagus spears, blanched
mature pecorino cheese, shaved
6 sprigs chervil
dressing
(3 parts olive oil to 1 part sherry vinegar, and a grinding of black pepper)

Base: place all ingredients in a food processor and pulse until the mixture resembles fine crumbs. Turn out into a bowl and knead lightly to form a ball of dough. Enclose dough in plastic wrap and refrigerate for 30 minutes.
Roll dough out on a lightly floured surface to 5mm thick. Prick well with a fork. Place on a tray lined with baking paper. Bake at 180°C for 15–20 minutes, until golden. Allow to cool on the baking tray.

Goose Egg Mixture: dice onion, place in a strainer and pour over 1 cup of boiling water. Turn onion on to a cloth and squeeze out excess liquid. Spread onion evenly over the cooked base.
Shell the eggs then chop them coarsely but evenly. Season with salt and pepper and mix in some chopped chives. Spread eggs evenly over onion. Cover with plastic wrap, pressing down firmly. Refrigerate for 30 minutes.

To assemble: remove plastic from egg mixture. Combine chives with mayonnaise and spread evenly over eggs. Cut the tart into 6 rectangles or triangles. Top each with 2 to 4 asparagus spears, shaved pecorino cheese and a sprig of chervil. Drizzle a little dressing around each tart.

Serves 6

Fleurieu Lamb

WITH LEMON, LEEK AND RISOTTO CAKE
AND CAPER AND VERDELHO VERJUICE SAUCE

Risotto Cake
1 leek (white part only), finely chopped
2 tablespoons unsalted butter
1 cup arborio rice
½ cup Verdelho verjuice
4 cups good chicken stock
zest and juice of ½ lemon
50g parmesan cheese, grated

Sauce
100ml Verdelho verjuice
100g small, salted capers, rinsed well
150ml rich meat glaze
(reduced lamb or beef stock)
250g cold, unsalted butter, diced

Lamb
1.5kg lamb loin, trimmed
1 tablespoon olive oil
salt and pepper
18 fresh sage leaves
oil for frying

Risotto Cake: sauté chopped leek in butter until soft. Add rice and cook over medium heat, stirring constantly, until rice is opaque.
Add verjuice and stir until well incorporated. Add warmed chicken stock, about 50ml at a time, stirring constantly.
Towards the end of cooking add lemon zest and juice. When rice is tender, remove from heat. Fold in parmesan. Check seasoning. Spread in a greased tray to set.

Sauce: Simmer verjuice and capers to reduce slowly and infuse flavours. Add glaze and reduce by ¼. Whisk in butter, about 25g at a time, until the sauce has emulsified and has a sheen (not all the butter may be necessary).

Lamb: cut lamb into 6 pieces. Heat oil in a pan. When hot, add lamb, season with salt and pepper and cook to medium-rare.
Rest lamb for 8–10 minutes in a warm place.

Fried sage leaves: Deep-fry sage leaves, a few at a time, until crisp. Drain on kitchen paper.

To assemble: cut risotto mixture into squares or rectangles and place on a greased baking tray. Bake at 180°C for about 15 minutes, until golden. Slice the lamb. Place a risotto cake on each warmed plate. Top with sliced lamb and coat with sauce. Garnish with fried sage leaves.

Serves 6

Victoria

Though relatively small in Australian terms, the state of Victoria has been blessed with enough different climates, landscapes and populations to ensure that it produces the most eclectic, diverse and enticing range of wines and the foods to go with them.

From the sophistication of Melbourne, a metropolitan Mecca for foodies whether eating out or browsing the markets, to the rural backwaters, a good bottle of wine and something interesting and authentic to eat is always close at hand.

Today, the Victorian wine industry – and its associated tourism – is a booming business, but it wasn't always so. Vines were first planted in Victoria during the gold rush days of the mid-1800s, but late in the century the state was blighted by phylloxera, a tiny aphid that dines on vine roots.

Many ruined vineyards were ripped out and not replaced, with farmers preferring to rely on other crops or livestock, and it wasn't until the 1960s and 1970s that Victoria really began to re-establish itself as a serious wine state.

Since then there has been a boom not only in vineyard development, but in regional food and wine consciousness. The key to this is Victoria's trump card – its diversity of regions. From the Alpine north, where steely dry Rieslings and sparkling wines are produced, to the cool-climate Yarra Valley and Mornington Peninsula, where Chardonnay and Pinot flourish; from the hilly Western ranges where elegant, peppery Shiraz is fermented, to the historic north-east of Rutherglen, where warmer temperatures produce some of the world's great fortified wines, Victoria has everything.

Victoria's other precious resource is its large and diverse population, many of whom arrived from southern Europe after Word War II with an ingrained taste for quality food and wine. This cross-cultural influence has inspired a truly innovative food culture and café society which is always looking for new culinary experiences, and a commitment to fine wine which now supports more than 200 cellar doors.

Whether you are indulging in stylish lunching on Melbourne's cosmopolitan Southbank or sipping a Muscat in a rustic tin shed with the rain drumming on the roof, Victoria is sure to excite your senses.

Melbourne's Southbank.

Local Yabbies

WITH A LEEK CUSTARD AND A GARNISH OF
SMOKED TROUT RILLETTE

Garlic and Leek Custard

    50g butter
    2 large leeks (green removed),
        quartered lengthwise, washed
    6 shallots, peeled, diced
    1 stalk celery, diced
    3 sprigs thyme, chopped
    30ml Pernod
    150ml stock (chicken or vegetable)
    300ml thickened cream
    4 large cloves confit garlic*
    3 whole eggs
    2 egg yolks
    salt and pepper

Melt butter without colouring. Add leeks,
shallots, celery and thyme. Cook on moderate
heat until vegetables are soft. Add Pernod and
flame to cook off alcohol.

Add stock and simmer for 5 minutes. Drain all
liquid from the vegetables and return vegetables
to the heat. Add cream. Simmer for 3 minutes.

Purée in a blender until fine. Add confit garlic
and purée for 1 minute. Pour mixture into a
bowl and allow to cool. Whisk in eggs and
yolks. Season with salt and pepper.

Grease 6 soufflé ramekins with butter or non-
stick spray. Fill each ramekin with custard
mixture to just below the lip.

Place the custards in a baking dish and fill it
with water to 2cm up the sides of the ramekins.
Lay a sheet of silicon paper over the ramekins
and seal the baking dish with a layer of foil.

Bake at 150°C for 40–45 minutes. To test for
readiness, insert a skewer into the middle of
custard. It should not be wet.

Yabbies

    30 live yabbies (small, fresh-water crayfish)
    olive oil
    salt and freshly ground black pepper

Keep live yabbies anaesthetised by layering
them with ice until ready to cook. Bring a large
pot of salted water to a rolling boil. Cook yabbies
on very high heat, 15 at a time, for 3 minutes.
Remove with a skimmer and place straight into
a large bowl of iced water.

Once cool, drain yabbies and shell 4 for each
serving. Using a small, sharp knife, remove
intestinal tract from cleaned yabbies. Using
sharp scissors, slit along the back of shells of
remaining yabbies. Peel back the shells a little.
Crack claws.

Smoked Trout Rillette

    1 sheet gelatine
        (or 1/2 teaspoon powdered gelatine)
    100ml fish stock, heated
    300g smoked trout, skinned and boned
    2 tablespoons soft butter
    salt and pepper

Soften leaf gelatine in cold water. Remove
gelatine and wring dry. (Or hydrate powdered
gelatine in 2 tablespoons of the cold fish
stock.) Add softened gelatine to hot fish stock
and stir until dissolved.

Flake smoked trout into a bowl, shredding it
into very small pieces with two forks.
Gradually add hot stock and continue to shred
the trout until it is very finely textured and
stock is absorbed. Allow to cool. When cool
add soft butter and combine well. (Note: if
trout is too warm the butter will melt and the
rillette will not set.) Season with salt and pepper
to taste. Refrigerate in a covered container.

Makes 6 (50g) servings.

To assemble: place all the yabbies on an oven
tray, drizzle with a little olive oil and season
with salt and pepper. Heat through in a very
hot oven for 5 minutes.

To serve: un-mould a leek custard on to each
plate. Place 4 peeled yabbies on top and 1
whole yabby resting against it.

The chef adds a little hot yabbie bisque, and
places a quenelle of cold Smoked Trout Rillette
on a piece of cucumber for height, with a few
fine potato crisps for texture.

*To make confit garlic gently heat whole,
peeled garlic cloves in olive oil until soft.
Remove from oil and cool.

Serves 6

RECIPE PREPARED BY
ALLA WOLF-TASKER
LAKE HOUSE RESTAURANT, DAYLESFORD

The undulating hills of the Macedon
Ranges, where the diverse attractions
of ancient Australian gums and
traditional English gardens dot the
landscape. The region is classic
sparkling wine country and a perfect
rural retreat only one and a half
hours from Melbourne.

WINE

*Hanging Rock Macedon
Cuvee VII*

Back in 1983, John Ellis
and the winemaking team at
Hanging Rock set out to make
a great Australian sparkling
wine. Today, they are up
to their seventh release of
'Macedon', a full-bodied and
powerful style, made using
wines from vintages between
1987 and 1996.

It is a perfect match for this
rich Lake House seafood dish.

Smoked Salmon on Grilled Cornbread

WITH STEAMED ASPARAGUS

600g sliced smoked salmon
400g washed rocket
18 asparagus spears, steamed
sea salt and cracked pepper
salmon roe
extra virgin olive oil
lime or lemon wedges
caper berries to garnish (optional)

Cornbread
3 cups fine cornmeal
3 cups milk
3 eggs
4 tablespoons olive oil
4 cooked corn cobs
1 1/2 cups plain flour
2 teaspoons baking soda
3 teaspoons baking powder
3 tablespoons brown sugar
sea salt and cracked pepper
a little olive oil for cooking

Cornbread: soak cornmeal in milk. Beat in eggs and 4 tablespoons of olive oil. Cut kernels from corn cobs and mix in. Add sifted dry ingredients. Pour into a greased, base-lined bread tin.
Bake at 180°C for 30 minutes or until golden brown. Turn out and cool.

To assemble: slice cooled cornbread 1cm thick. Grease a hot fry-pan or grill-pan with olive oil and lightly brown cornbread slices.
Place a slice of cornbread in the centre of each plate. Top with smoked salmon and rocket. Season steamed asparagus. Place 3 asparagus spears on top. Arrange a little salmon roe around each stack and drizzle with olive oil. Garnish with lime or lemon wedges and caper berries if you like.

Serves 6

RECIPE PREPARED BY
ADAM SOLTAN
COPE-WILLIAMS WINERY AND
COUNTRY CLUB

A visit to the Cope-Williams Winery and Country Club could almost be a trip into the English countryside. Classic country gardens, fine buildings and even a friendly game of cricket on a Saturday morning combine to give the estate a heady, pastoral atmosphere. After 20 years on the property, Judy Cope-Williams has a garden which is the envy of locals and tourists alike.

WINE

Cope-Williams Romsey
Another classic example of the great sparkling wines that can be produced in the ideal cool climate of the Macedon Ranges. Aged for two years, Romsey is a full-bodied, ripe style with a lovely long finish. Wonderful with smoked salmon.

Tian of Crab

200ml mayonnaise
380g cooked blue swimmer crab meat
cayenne, salt and pepper
juice of 1–2 limes
20 basil leaves, julienned
Tomato Petals Confit (recipe follows)
2 avocados
salt, white pepper and lemon juice
100ml Gazpacho Sauce (recipe follows)

Mix together the mayonnaise, crab meat, the seasonings, lime juice and basil.

Use the mixture to fill 4 tian moulds (each 5cm high, 5cm diameter), placing tomato 'petals' in the bottom, middle and on top. Allow 12 'petals' for each mould.

Peel avocados and cut flesh into small dice, or purée. Season with salt, pepper and lemon juice.

To serve: un-mould a tian in the middle of each plate. Place a small mound of diced avocado or quenelle of puréed avocado on top of each tian and surround with Gazpacho Sauce.

Serves 4 as an entrée

Tomato Petals Confit

Blanch roma tomatoes and peel. Cut tomatoes in halves, lengthwise. Lay halves on a foil-lined tray. Sprinkle with Maldon sea salt and chopped thyme. Leave in a low oven overnight to semi-dry. Once dry cut out 5cm round tomato 'petals'.

Gazpacho Sauce

6 roma tomatoes
200ml tomato sauce
10 drops Tabasco sauce
300ml extra virgin olive oil
salt and pepper

Purée tomatoes, sauce and Tabasco in blender. Drizzle in oil to emulsify. Pass through a fine sieve. Season.

A quirky fish café sign in Melbourne's St Kilda, home to a thriving bar, restaurant and nightlife scene.

RECIPE PREPARED BY
MICHAEL LAMBIE AND PAUL KNIGHT
CIRCA, THE PRINCE
ST KILDA

WINE

Diamond Valley Estate 1997 Chardonnay
From Diamond Valley Vineyards in the Yarra Valley, this tangy-fresh Chardonnay has a complex bouquet with attractive nectarine and peach fruit flavours and very subtle oak. Recommended by staff at Circa in St Kilda to accompany their crab tian.

An Array of Seafood

For steaming

 12 fresh black mussels
 2 large blue swimmer crabs
 1 clove garlic
 1 cup white wine
 sprig of parsley

Batter

 3 eggs
 1 cup self-raising flour
 pinch of salt and pepper
 1 cup beer

For frying

 4 potatoes, cut into french fries
 2 calamari tubes, cut into rings
 8 medium-sized green prawns
 8 scallops
 4 flathead fillets, cut in halves
 flour
 vegetable oil

To serve au naturel

 8 fresh Tasmanian oysters in the shell
 4 cooked king prawns
 50g mesclun
 lemon wedges and parsley

For steaming: heat a pan and add mussels, crabs, garlic, wine and parsley. Cover until mussels are steamed open. Drain and cool.

Batter: beat eggs and fold in flour, salt and pepper. Stir in beer.

For frying: heat oil to 180°C and deep-fry potatoes. Remove and drain on absorbent paper. Dust with flour all seafood for frying, then dip in batter to coat. Fry in hot oil until golden brown. Drain on absorbent paper.

To assemble: take a large platter and place mesclun on one half. Arrange oysters, prawns, mussels and crabs on top. Place the chips on the other half of the platter and top with fried seafood. Garnish with lemon and parsley. Serve Tartare Sauce and Cocktail Sauce separately.

Tartare Sauce

 Mix together: 1/2 cup mayonnaise; 1 large gherkin, finely chopped; 1 tablespoon drained capers, chopped; 2 teaspoons chopped parsley; 1/2 teaspoon lemon juice and 1/4 teaspoon Worcestershire sauce.

Cocktail Sauce

 Mix together: 1/2 cup mayonnaise; 1/4 cup sherry; 5 drops Tabasco sauce; 1/4 cup tomato sauce.

RECIPE PREPARED BY
FRANCESCA MIGNANI
LILLYDALE INTERNATIONAL, LILLYDALE

WINE

Kellybrook 2000 Riesling Seafood and Riesling are natural partners, which is why the subtle floral nose and crisp acidity of this Kellybrook 2000 Riesling makes it the ideal complement to this stunning array of shellfish, calamari and flathead.

Situated on the edge of the region in Wonga Park, Kellybrook is not only the oldest licence in the Yarra Valley, it is also the closest winery to Melbourne. The winery, cellar door and function centre/restaurant overlook the 20-acre vineyard, which nestles in a fertile basin.

When French Champagne house Moet & Chandon decided to expand into the global sparkling wine market in 1985, they chose this breathtaking spot in the Yarra Valley to build their Australian winery. The striking cellar door offers sweeping views of the Yarra, the Domain Chandon Vineyards (top) and the valley overlooking St Hubert's Vineyard (bottom), here showing off the last of its fertile, green shades as the season swings into mid-November.

Antipasti

INCLUDING YARRA VALLEY DAIRY BRIE,
YARRA VALLEY SALMON ROE, BUFFALO CABANOS
FROM ST ANDREWS, MIXED VEGETABLE PICKLE
AND CRUSTY BREAD

PREPARED BY
BRETT METHERALL
DOMAINE CHANDON AUSTRALIA
YARRA VALLEY

WINE

Chandon Brut

In the tasting room at Domain Chandon, visitors can not only sample the brilliant array of sparkling wines for which the company is famous, but also try the flavours of the Yarra with an antipasti plate. The Chandon Brut, made from Pinot Noir and Chardonnay, has lifted fruit and fig aromas with floral notes, flavours of white peach, honey and roasted nuts and a refreshing finish.

The De Bortolis have been making wine in Australia since 1928 in Griffith and are one of the nation's great family winery names. Leanne De Bortoli and husband Steve Webber have been running the award-winning De Bortoli Yarra Valley Winery and Restaurant since 1987, where the Italian-influenced food is based on local produce.

The wine list offers a broad tasting experience, from full-bodied Cabernet and Shiraz to small-lot, experimental varietals driven by microclimate and terroir and the famously luscious Noble One botrytised dessert wine.

RECIPES PREPARED BY
NEIL WOODLEY
DE BORTOLI WINERY &
RESTAURANT

Saffron Angel Hair Pasta

TOSSED WITH SCALLOPS AND
JULIENNE VEGETABLES

Julienne Vegetables
  1 medium-sized carrot
  1 medium-sized zucchini
  1 red capsicum, de-seeded
  2 stalks celery

  400g saffron angel hair pasta

  2 tablespoons good quality olive oil
  2 cloves garlic, very finely chopped
  16 scallops
  1/4 cup white wine
  salt and pepper

  Trim vegetables and cut into fine matchstick strips.
  Cook and drain pasta.
  Heat olive oil in a pan and add garlic. Quickly sear scallops (60 seconds each side). Add wine, salt and pepper to taste and the julienne vegetables. Cook for 4 minutes then gently add the cooked saffron pasta.

Serves 4

Cervo con Morenere

MEDALLIONS OF YARRA VALLEY VENISON
WITH BLACKBERRIES, SERVED WITH SEMOLINA
AND PARMESAN TORTONI

Semolina and Parmesan Tortoni
  4 cups milk
  3 tablespoons butter
  zest of lemon
  2 1/4 cups semolina
  3 eggs
  1 1/2 cups grated parmesan
  salt and white pepper
  extra butter
  4 tablespoons cream
  extra grated parmesan

Venison
  olive oil
  4–6 venison medallions, each 50g
  about 12 blackberries
  red wine
  100ml beef jus or stock

  Tortoni: put milk, butter and lemon zest in a saucepan and bring to the boil. Slowly add semolina, stirring constantly. Cook for 3 minutes. Mix together eggs, parmesan, salt and pepper. Add to semolina mixture. Roll into logs in buttered foil. Chill for 2 hours. Cut into 2cm lengths and place in a buttered baking dish. Drizzle with cream and sprinkle with extra parmesan. Bake at 200°C for 12–15 minutes.

  Venison: heat oil in a pan and sear venison medallions for about 2 minutes each side. Set aside to rest in a warm place. Deglaze the pan with a little red wine. Add beef jus and blackberries. Reduce to coating consistency and check seasoning. Return venison to the pan, warm through and serve immediately with semolina tortoni.

Serves 2

WINE

De Bortoli 1999 Yarra Valley Gewurztraminer
This lively Gewurztraminer, with its floral scents and spicy notes, makes a good match for the scallops and pasta combination. A refreshing change from Chardonnay, which would also go well with this dish.

WINE

De Bortoli 1998 Yarra Valley Cabernet Sauvignon
The 1998 vintage produced reds with excellent colour and fruit concentration. This Cabernet has a typically complex nose with tobacco and macerated fruit characters. The palate has very soft integrated fruit and oak flavours. A Jimmy Watson Memorial Trophy Winner, this wine will mature and age gracefully over 5–10 years.

Caramel Panna Cotta

WITH CHOCOLATE SORBET AND TANGELO SYRUP

500ml whipping cream
150g caster sugar
2 1/2 leaves gelatine
   (or 1 1/2 teaspoons powdered gelatine)

Heat cream in a saucepan to just below boiling point. Remove from heat.

Place sugar in a large saucepan over a full heat and stir until it has all melted.

Continue to cook the sugar until it turns a pale golden caramel colour – not too dark or it will taste burnt. When it reaches the desired colour immediately take off the heat.

Very carefully add cream, a little at a time, until it is all incorporated. Bring back to the boil, stirring, then remove from heat.

Soak leaf gelatine in cold water for 3–4 minutes until soft then drain and squeeze out water. Add to hot cream. (Or hydrate powdered gelatine in 1–2 tablespoons cold water, then dissolve by heating in the microwave for about 30 seconds. Add to hot cream.) Pour into 4 moulds and refrigerate to set.

Chocolate Sorbet
   115g dark chocolate, chopped
   45g sugar
   45ml water
   200ml water

Melt the chocolate. Dissolve the sugar in the 45ml of water then stir in melted chocolate. Add remaining water. Cool. Churn in an ice cream machine and place in the freezer.

Tangelo Syrup
   500g tangelos
   150g sugar
   150ml water

Reserve 1 tangelo for segments. Cut the rest into quarters and place in a pot. Add sugar and water. Simmer for 1 1/2 –2 hours. Liquidise then pass through sieve. Adjust with water to make a pouring consistency.

To assemble: peel and segment the remaining tangelo.

To turn out Panna Cotta place each mould in hot water for a few seconds then invert on a plate (aim for the centre), and lightly tap the mould until the dessert drops out.

Drizzle Tangelo Syrup around each Panna Cotta, add a scoop of Chocolate Sorbet and finish with 3–4 tangelo segments.

Serves 4

(For the Panna Cotta pictured the chef has lined the base of the mould with a layer of caramelised sugar as in Crème Caramel.)

RECIPE PREPARED BY
TIMOTHY FOX
YERING STATION WINE BAR

WINE

Barak's Bridge 1999 Botrytis Semillon
This wine is made from Botrytis-infected Semillon grapes sourced from Griffith, the home of the 'sticky'. The wine shows beautifully balanced acid and sugar levels with ripe varietal fruit flavours, supported by hints of cedary French oak.
A memorable complement to Caramel Panna Cotta.

Established in 1988, Yering Station is one of the major wine producers in the Yarra Valley. Producing premium quality wines under both the Yering Station and Barak's Bridge labels, the new facilities are a must-see when visiting the Yarra Valley. Linger over the stunning views, taste the extensive selection of wines on offer and then enjoy the cuisine in the sparkling new restaurant.

Kangaroo Fillet

WITH ROASTED BEETROOT AND ONION WEDGES
AND A REDCURRANT JUS

2 plump, fresh beetroot
2 spanish onions
olive oil
balsamic vinegar
freshly ground black pepper
sea salt
1 cup reduced veal stock
1/2 cup red wine
1 tablespoon redcurrant jelly
1kg kangaroo fillets
4 cups baby spinach

Peel beetroot and onions and slice into wedges. Place in a roasting dish and coat with oil, vinegar, pepper and salt. Roast at 160°C for 45 minutes, tossing occasionally.

For the jus, simmer stock, wine and redcurrant jelly until slightly thickened.

Clean kangaroo fillets of all sinew and cut into serving-size portions. On a very hot grill-pan or pan, sear kangaroo then place on a roasting tray. Finish in the oven at 160°C for 3–4 minutes to cook to very rare.

Blanch baby spinach to wilt. Drain well.

To serve: place spinach on each plate with beetroot and onion wedges. Spoon 2 tablespoons of the jus over the vegetables. Slice kangaroo and arrange around the plate and dust with freshly ground black pepper.

Serves 4

RECIPE PREPARED BY
ANN MAUVER AND HEDDA DOOLEY
THE YARRA GLEN GRAND HOTEL
YARRA VALLEY

WINE

Yarra Glen Cabernet Sauvignon
This is the essence of Australia — the rich red colours and flavours of beetroot and rare kangaroo, enhanced by the subtle oak flavours and rich berry fruit of a Yarra Glen Cabernet Sauvignon.

The heritage-listed Yarra Glen Grand Hotel was built in 1888 and continues to be one of the region's most significant landmarks, symbolising the history and spirit of the Yarra Valley. The perfect stopover, it provides everything from a modern front bar to slake a traveller's thirst to classically decorated upstairs bedrooms and a dining room that serves the best in local produce and wine.

Salmon with Fresh Salad

Established in 1976, the Lillydale restaurant and cellar door is set among 33 acres of vineyard which have been developed by the historic Australian wine company McWilliam's.

The cook-your-own barbecue experience reflects the casual elegance implied in the restaurant décor; a salmon cutlet sears on the charcoal grill, while a fresh salad awaits.

PREPARED BY
MCWILLIAM'S LILLYDALE VINEYARDS
BARBECUE RESTAURANT

WINE

Lillydale Vineyards 1998 Chardonnay
This wine shows ripe, intense melon and tropical fruit aromas enhanced by a very delicate trace of nutty French oak and buttery characters. A medium-oaked palate with a long, crisp finish makes it the wine of choice with this delicate salmon cutlet.

The bright green new vine leaves light up McWilliam's Lillydale vineyards in springtime.

Seared Fillet of Swordfish

SERVED ON ROASTED CORN, RED PEPPER AND
AVOCADO SALSA

Salsa
   2 fresh corn cobs, husks on
   2 red capsicums
   1 avocado
   1 tablespoons chopped fresh coriander
   50ml balsamic vinegar
   30ml olive oil
   salt and pepper

Swordfish
   2 portions of swordfish fillet, each 200g
   a little oil

Salsa: Roast corn cobs until the husks turn black. Peel off husks then slice kernels from the cobs.

Roast capsicums then de-seed, peel and cut into dice. Peel, stone and dice avocado.

In a bowl combine corn, capsicum and avocado with coriander, vinegar, olive oil, salt and pepper. Toss until well mixed.

Swordfish: Lightly oil swordfish. Sear on a very hot char-grill or cast-iron ridged grill-pan for 1–2 minutes each side. Turn fish at right angles on the grill half way through searing each side to give criss-cross marking.

To serve: arrange salsa on each plate. Place swordfish on top. Drizzle remaining salsa over the fish. Garnish with chives.

Serves 2

RECIPE PREPARED BY
RUSSELL BALD
WILLOW CREEK VINEYARD RESTAURANT

Winemaker Simon Black has been producing premium Mornington Peninsula wines at Willow Creek since 1989. His Tulum range, in particular, is hard to find in bottleshops, which makes the trip to the cellar door a must. The new state-of-the-art winery was finished in time for the 1998 vintage and provides an interesting insight for visitors who want to learn more about the craft.

WINE

Willow Creek 1998 Tulum Chardonnay

The Tulum 1998 Chardonnay is fermented in French oak barriques, giving it fine structure and balance. It has a clean bouquet and a complex, powerful palate with grapefruit and melon flavours, and is an ideal accompaniment to swordfish fillet.

Stuffed Leg of Farmed Rabbit

WITH FRESH ARTICHOKE HEARTS IN WHITE WINE

Stuffed Rabbit
  2 hind legs of farmed rabbit
  12–16 sultanas
  12–16 pine nuts
  Italian (flat-leaf) parsley
  olive oil
  2 cloves garlic, peeled, chopped
  200ml white wine
  2 teaspoons tomato purée or paste
  1 cup rabbit or veal stock
  salt and pepper

With a sharp paring knife make a small incision between the inside leg muscles and enlarge it slightly with your finger. Into each leg place 6–8 sultanas, 6–8 pine nuts and 10–12 good sized parsley leaves.

Lightly cook garlic in a little oil in a heavy-based pan. Add rabbit and lightly brown on both sides. Add wine and allow to evaporate slightly. Reduce heat. Add tomato purée or paste and stock. Simmer gently for 35–40 minutes. Do not overcook or the meat will fall off the bones. Season to taste.

Serve hot with cooking juices.

Fresh Artichoke Hearts in White Wine
  8 fresh young (small) artichokes
  50ml good olive oil
  2 green garlic tips
  100ml dry white unwooded wine
  Italian parsley
  salt and pepper

Trim fresh artichokes down to the hearts. Make a stock of the discarded leaves and stalks. Strain stock and set aside.

In a heavy-based pan heat the oil and green garlic tips. Add artichokes and sear quickly. Add wine and allow to partly evaporate. Gradually add artichoke stock and allow to simmer with lid on. (Artichokes should be semi-immersed in liquid, not completely covered.) Artichokes are very thirsty (dry) vegetables and need a lot of stock. Be patient, adding a little stock at a time, until the artichokes are sufficiently steamed. Gentle cooking time: 30–40 minutes. Season to taste. Towards the end of cooking, add freshly plucked parsley (un-chopped).

Serves 2

RECIPE PREPARED BY
GENNARO MAZZELLA
GENNARO'S TABLE, VILLA PRIMAVERA

WINE

Villa Primavera 1998 Pinot Noir

Gennaro Mazzella established Villa Primavera in 1984 and soon after launched his Italian farmhouse-style restaurant, Gennaro's Table. A consistent winner of tourism and food awards, it provides a very special Italian dining experience. Gennaro's Pinot Noir is the perfect partner to his rabbit dish, displaying typical strawberry and plum characters with fine acidity.

The surf beaches of Port Phillip Bay that run along the Mornington Peninsula coastline provide cooling breezes to steady ripening in the region's vineyards. The quaint seaside town Portsea, at the tip of the peninsula, is home to some of the most expensive real estate in Victoria and is also immortalised as the place where Prime Minister Harold Holt lost his life while swimming in the 1960s.

Pere al Formaggio

TUSCAN STUFFED PEAR WITH ROCKET, CHEESE
AND PINE NUTS, SERVED ON A BED OF ROCKET SALAD

2 Red Hill josephine pears
   (or ripe pears of your choice)

Filling
   1/2 cup rocket leaves
   20g (1 1/2 tablespoons) pine nuts
   1/3 shallot, peeled
   75g mascarpone
   75g Philadelphia cream cheese
   1 lemon
   salt and pepper

Salad
   2 cups rocket leaves
   pinch of sea salt
   30ml extra virgin olive oil
   5ml (1 teaspoon) aged balsamic vinegar
   fine julienne of red capsicum for garnish

Filling: roughly chop the rocket, nuts and shallot
and mix together. Soften mascarpone and cream
cheese and combine with rocket mixture. Add
juice of half the lemon. Season to taste.

Pears: cut each pear in half. Scoop out the
core to leave a generous well in the centre.
Rub the pears with the remaining half lemon.
Fill pear halves with the rocket/cheese mixture
and neatly smooth off excess. Cover and refrigerate until required.

Salad: in a bowl, sprinkle sea salt over rocket
and toss with olive oil and balsamic vinegar.
Divide into 4 serving plates.

To serve: cut the pear halves in two lengthwise.
Present 2 pear quarters on each salad.
   Garnish with very fine julienne of red capsicum.

Serves 4

RECIPE PREPARED BY
MAX PAGANONI
MAX'S AT RED HILL ESTATE
MORNINGTON PENINSULA

*The Mornington Peninsula is a
wonderful retreat with many special
winery and cellar door experiences,
from the smart, sleek Red Hill
Estate with Max's modern cooking
to the shady forest retreat of
Tanglewood Downs.*

*Tanglewood is an evocative place
to taste award-winning Pinot and
Cabernet Sauvignon made by Ken
and Wendy Bilham. The wooden
hut, built in the mid-1900s, is
sometimes the venue for jazz
evenings.*

WINE
Red Hill Estate 2000 Sauvignon Blanc
*A medium yellow-green colour with a
pronounced varietal bouquet, the 2000
Sauvignon Blanc has a lively, crisp palate
which suits the subtle flavours of this
Tuscan-influenced dish.*

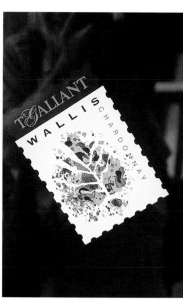

Antipasti

INCLUDING PROSCIUTTO, SALAMI, CORNICHONS,
CUPRESE, ROASTED CAPSICUMS, ONION CONFIT
WITH OLIVES, CHICK PEA SALAD, BALSAMIC
MUSHROOM SALAD AND TOMATO
AND FRESH BOCCONCINI

PLATTER PREPARED BY
LA BARACCA TRATTORIA
T'GALLANT

WINE

T'Gallant 2000 Imogen Pinot Gris

*Opulent and slightly more alcoholic than
the Pinot Grigio, the Imogen Pinot Gris
follows an Alsatian style with hints of spice,
a higher degree of richness and
an intense peach flavour.*

---

*Husband and wife winemakers Kevin McCarthy
and Kathleen Quealy have taken the spicy, flinty
Italian white variety Pinot Grigio (and its French
alter ego Pinot Gris) under their wing and are
producing very good examples of each style, along
with a popular Pinot Noir and Holystone rosé.
The winery's restaurant, La Baracca Trattoria,
is open for lunch seven days.*

Originals of the T'Gallant labels, based on works of art by local artist Ken Cato, are displayed in the winery's cellar door.

Atlantic Salmon Fillet

WITH MANGO AND MINT SAUCE

Mango and Mint Sauce
 2 mangoes
 1/2 bunch mint
 1 red onion, peeled
 1 teaspoon brown sugar
 olive oil
 lemon juice

Caramelised Lemon Garnish
 6 lemons
 1 cup sugar
 3/4 cup water

Salmon and Potatoes
 8 chat (baby new) potatoes
 olive oil and butter
 salt and pepper
 4 portions salmon fillet, each 180g

Mint and Mango Sauce: peel and dice mangoes. Cut mint into fine julienne. Finely chop red onion. Mix together mangoes, mint, onion and brown sugar. Splash in some olive oil and lemon juice and mix. Leave at room temperature for 2 hours to infuse.

Caramelised Lemon: peel the lemons then cut peel into thin matchstick strips. Place lemon peel in a pan with sugar and water. Boil until the mixture is reduced to a syrup – about 10 minutes. Cool.

Salmon and Potatoes: bring whole potatoes to a boil. Refresh then slice into 1–2cm pieces. Heat olive oil and butter in a pan. Season potatoes and sauté.

Season salmon fillets then sear them in a frypan. Put the pan and salmon in the oven at 180°C for 6–8 minutes The salmon should be barely cooked through and pink in the middle. Remove salmon from the oven and let rest on a warm area for 3–4 minutes.

To serve: place salmon on a bed of sautéed potatoes and salad greens, top with the sauce and garnish with caramelised lemon.

Serves 4

RECIPE PREPARED BY
ALEX SOCHA
THE MORNING STAR ESTATE
WINERY & BISTRO

Arguably Mornington Peninsula's most exciting new development, Morning Star Estate was originally a Catholic boys' home and is now being turned into a five-star restaurant, hotel and function centre. The building above is one of the first to be restored to its original grandeur. Owner Judy Barrett has planted 50,000 roses which will provide a perfumed pathway as visitors wander down the sloping property to the sea. A must-see in the Mornington Peninsula.

WINE

Morning Star Estate 1995 Pinot Noir
Fragrant strawberry and cherry fruit aromas are faithfully repeated on the palate of this medium-bodied, delicate Pinot Noir. These subtle varietal flavours complement perfectly the fine flavours of baked salmon.

Tagliolini con il Grancho

HOMEMADE TAGLIOLINI WITH SNOW CRAB

Crab Stock
  1 small onion, finely chopped
  1 clove garlic, peeled, crushed
  olive oil
  crab shells
  1 bay leaf
  peppercorns

Tagliolini
  400g strong, durum wheat flour
  4 eggs

  6 snow crabs
  1 clove garlic
  3 tablespoons olive oil
  250ml crab stock
  1 tablespoon finely chopped parsley
  salt

Crab Stock: Sauté onion and garlic in a little oil until onion softens. Add crab shells and toss for a few minutes. Cover with water, add bay leaf and peppercorns, and simmer for 20 minutes. Strain stock through a fine sieve.

Tagliolini: place flour in a large bowl, making a well in the centre. Add eggs and work into a soft dough. Let it rest for 30 minutes. Roll out by hand, or using a pasta machine, roll to the finest setting. Cut into thin strips, or use tagliolini cutter on pasta machine. Let pasta rest until needed.

WINE

Di Stasio 1999 Chardonnay
Café Di Stasio in St Kilda produces its own label Chardonnay from fruit sourced in the Yarra Valley. Lively and well balanced, with good varietal definition, it is a good match with John Snelling's pasta and snow crab recipe, and very good value.

Snow Crabs: add crabs to a large pot of boiling water and poach for 10 minutes. Drain and cool until easy to handle. Remove all edible meat from the crab bodies and claws.

Make sauce by sautéing garlic in a pan with olive oil. Add half the crab meat and gently cook for a few minutes. Add stock and simmer until reduced by half.

Cook tagliolini in a large pot of boiling, salted water until al dente (it cooks very quickly). Drain and add to crab sauce.

Add remaining crab meat and parsley and toss.

To serve: arrange twirls of tagliolini on plates.

Serves 6

RECIPE PREPARED BY
JOHN SNELLING
CAFÉ DI STASIO, ST KILDA

Winding wrought iron vines adorn a Victorian window.

Honey Crunch Ice Cream

WITH TOASTED GINGERBREAD, ROASTED—CINNAMON
OIL AND SUGAR SWIRLS

Honeycomb

> 30ml honey
> 30ml golden syrup
> 3/4 cup caster sugar
> 30ml water
> 1 1/4 teaspoons baking soda

Boil honey, golden syrup, sugar and water in a saucepan to hard crack stage (test by putting a few drops into cold water). Beat in baking soda until it foams up. Immediately pour the mixture on to a cold slab or metal tray. Once cool, break honeycomb up and store air-tight in the freezer.

Roasted-Cinnamon Oil

> 250g cinnamon bark
> 300g cinnamon powder
> 1 litre pure olive oil

Roast cinnamon bark in a hot oven until fragrant. Blend cinnamon bark and powder in a processor with 1/2 cup of oil until pasty. Add remaining oil. Seal in airtight jars for 2 weeks, turning them every 2 days. Then pass the oil through coffee filters until clear.

Gingerbread

> 150g unsalted butter
> 250g brown sugar
> 350g treacle
> 200ml milk
> 430g plain flour
> 1/2 teaspoon salt
> 2 teaspoons baking powder
> 1 teaspoon ground ginger
> 1 teaspoon ground allspice
> 1 egg, beaten

Melt butter with sugar and treacle. Add milk to warm slightly. Add sifted dry ingredients to liquids. Beat for 2 minutes. Add egg and beat until smooth. Turn mixture into a greased, standard loaf tin. (It should come 5/6 of the way up the tin.)

Bake at 160°C for 1 1/2 hours. Cool on a wire rack.

Slice cool gingerbread lengthwise, about 3mm thick (best to use a bread-slicer). Cut out rounds, 10–12cm diameter. Toast in a hot oven. Cool and store air-tight.

WINE

Chambers Rosewood Special Muscat
One of the wonderfully complex Muscats for which Rutherglen is justly famous, Chambers' Rosewood is a rich and raisiny mouthful. Intense dried fruit flavours and an almost savoury maltiness combine to give a luscious wine with a fine, clean finish. Perfect with pudding or cheese.

Honey Crunch Ice Cream

> 24 egg yolks
> 150g sugar
> 300g honey
> 1 litre milk
> 1 litre cream
> 150g honeycomb, broken into small fragments

Combine egg yolks, sugar and honey in a heat-proof bowl. Bring milk to the boil and pour over yolk mixture, whisking vigorously. Place bowl over hot water and cook, stirring, until custard coats the back of the spoon. Strain into another bowl over ice to cool rapidly. Chill.

Add cream to cold custard then churn in an ice cream machine (follow manufacturer's instructions). Once frozen, place a layer of ice cream in a tub and top with a layer of crumbled honeycomb. Repeat layers until all are used up. Refreeze.

To serve: place a smear of double cream in each chilled dessert dish. Place a round of gingerbread on the cream. Top with a small scoop of ice cream. Repeat with another disc of gingerbread and scoop of ice cream.
Spoon 15ml of cinnamon oil around. Add some honeycomb fragments.
The chef adds a sugar swirl garnish.

Serves 12

RECIPE PREPARED BY
BRENDAN MCQUEEN
EZARD AT ADELPHI, MELBOURNE

Even in the international hubbub of Melbourne's metropolis, native flowers remind residents of a rural past.

Chicken and Shiitake Mushroom Terrine

3 x1kg free-range chickens
1 tablespoon each chopped chives, chervil, parsley, tarragon
40 shallots, peeled
100g butter
salt and pepper
cayenne pepper
100ml white wine
4 cloves garlic, peeled, chopped
2kg shiitake mushrooms
1 litre chicken stock
4 bunches baby leeks
8 egg whites
8 leaves gelatine
   (or 4 teaspoons powdered gelatine)
50ml truffle oil to serve

De-bone the chickens from the backbone, keeping skin intact. Remove legs and wings, all sinew and excess fat. Free the breast from the skin.

Place the chopped herbs between the skin and breast and pat down.

Finely chop shallots. Sweat half the shallots in 50g of butter until soft. Drain off the butter and allow to cool.

Season chickens with salt, pepper and cayenne. Cover the breasts with the cooked shallots then splash over the wine. Refrigerate overnight.

Sweat remaining shallots and garlic in 50g butter. Remove mushrooms stalks (reserve for clarification). Add mushrooms to shallots. Add chicken stock. Cover, and cook gently until mushrooms are soft. Strain, reserving the stock. Allow both to cool.

Trim baby leeks. Cook until soft. Refresh in iced water. Drain.

Place chickens, skin sides down, in a terrine mould (40cm long). Press into the corners, leaving the skin hanging over the sides. Add a layer of mushrooms, then leeks. Repeat layers, finishing with mushrooms. Overlap skin to cover the filling. Cover terrine with foil.

Bring a water bath to the boil and put in the terrine. Cook in the oven at 160°C for 1 1/2 hours.

To make a clarification, thoroughly blend shiitake stalks and egg whites. Whisk this into the cold, reserved mushroom stock and bring to the boil, whisking all the time.

A raft will form on top of the stock. Allow to simmer for 10 minutes.

Meanwhile, soak gelatine leaves in water. (Or hydrate powdered gelatine in 2–3 tablespoons cold water, then dissolve by standing over hot water.) Strain the hot stock through a muslin cloth (stock should be crystal clear). Season and add drained gelatine leaves (or dissolved powdered gelatine).

Remove terrine from the water bath and gently pour out the liquid. Allow to cool, then pour in the stock. Refrigerate overnight before unmoulding.

Slice, using a long, sharp knife. Serve dressed with a little truffle oil.

Serves 12–14

RECIPE PREPARED BY
DONOVAN COOKE
EST. EST. EST., MELBOURNE

WINE

Mooroduc Estate 1998 Wild Yeast Chardonnay

A restrained and complex wine with elegance and grace. Subtle varietal flavours are supported by nuttiness from the wild yeast ferment, making it forthright enough to complement the light chicken and mushroom terrine.

Brown Brothers of Milawa is a Victorian favourite, with an unbroken 111 year history of making wine. The company's dedication to experimentation and innovation has given the Brown Bros label national and international significance.

The Epicurean Centre was built in 1994 so that Brown Brothers wines would be complemented by locally grown produce. Each dish is painstakingly designed to reflect the flavour profile of the wines.

WINES

Brown Brothers 1999 Barbera
The bouquet of this Italian varietal is rich and spicy, while the palate is pleasantly savoury with a soft tannin finish, ideal as an accompaniment to the richness of roast duck.

Brown Brothers 2000 Moscato
How better to follow than with this luscious dessert wine with surprisingly lively grapey fruit and a spritz on the palate, its intense fruit complementing the panna cotta perfectly.

Vanilla Bean Panna Cotta

WITH ORANGE SYRUP AND MARINATED STRAWBERRIES

300ml cream (35% milk fat)
1/2 vanilla bean (pod)
1 cinnamon stick
rind of 1/4 lemon
rind of 1/4 orange
2 coffee beans
150g palm sugar
300ml mascarpone
2 gelatine leaves
     (or 1 teaspoon powdered gelatine)

Orange Syrup
300g sugar
300ml water
rind of 1 orange, cut into fine shreds

500g strawberries

Warm cream with vanilla bean, cinnamon, rinds, coffee beans and palm sugar. To infuse flavours let it stand for 30 minutes. Add the mascarpone, stir then strain.

Place gelatine leaves in cold water until soft, squeeze out water and add to warm cream mixture. (Or hydrate powdered gelatine in 2 tablespoons cold water then gently warm over boiling water to dissolve. Add to cream mixture.)

Pour into 8 individual cooled, oiled moulds. Refrigerate overnight to allow to set.

Orange Syrup: dissolve sugar in water by warming on the stove top. As it cools add orange rind. Cool overnight.

To serve: wash strawberries and toss in orange syrup. Turn out panna cotta by dipping moulds in hot water for a few seconds, or lifting panna cotta from the sides of moulds.

Arrange on serving plates with strawberries in orange syrup. Garnish with green strawberry leaves, if anything.

Serves 8

RECIPES PREPARED BY
CHRIS LEE AND JESSIE GALLAGHER
MILAWA EPICUREAN CENTRE
BROWN BROTHERS VINEYARD, MILAWA

Free Range Roast Duck

WITH UDON NOODLES

2kg duck (free range if available)
300ml walnut oil
70ml sesame oil
3 star anise
3 dried red chillies, chopped
2 tablespoons chopped white spring onion
2 knobs of ginger, sliced
4 cloves garlic, peeled, sliced
70ml yellow rice wine
500ml chicken stock
150ml unsalted, dark soy sauce
50g rock sugar, crushed
750g udon noodles
16 baby bok choy plants

Cut the duck into 8 large pieces without deboning. Score skin and fat in a diamond pattern.

Heat walnut oil and fry duck pieces until golden on all sides. Remove and place on kitchen paper in a warm place.

In a heavy pot, heat sesame oil with star anise, dried chillies, spring onion, sliced ginger and garlic. Stir and fry until it smokes. Add duck. Flame with rice wine. Cook off alcohol. Then add stock and bring to the boil. Skim off residue then simmer for about 1 hour.

Add soy sauce and return to a simmer. The meat is ready when it pulls away easily from the bone; liquids should have reduced by 2/3.

At the last minute add rock sugar and cook until meat is glazed.

Prepare noodles as per packet directions.
Blanch bok choy in boiling water, drain well.

To serve: place warm noodles, bok choy and duck portions on serving plates with the liquids reduced to a glaze.

Serves 8

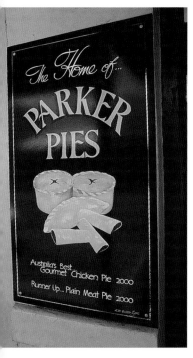

Rutherglen

Flat and dry, the landscape of the Rutherglen area in North East Victoria has provided the perfect terroir for producing an outstanding range of luscious fortifieds and richly flavoured table wines for more than 150 years.

The mainstay of the region, and the most compelling reason to visit, has always been its world-class aged Muscats and Tokays, deliciously decadent, multi-layered fortified wines with intensely rich and complex flavours of dried fruit, nuts, spice and Christmas pudding. Sherry and port styles from here, too, are virtually matchless; only a few Barossa examples come even remotely close. In recent years, though, Rutherglen's table wines have also started to attract more attention, especially its big, ripe Shiraz and Durif reds, built for long ageing.

Mount Prior has been making premium table wines since 1860.

The pace of life is pretty slow in the country around Rutherglen, making it a perfect escape from the more hectic pace in metropolitan Melbourne.

Eye Fillet of Beef

WITH CARAMELISED ONION SOUFFLÉ, CRACKED BLACK
PEPPER REDUCTION AND SPRING VEGETABLES

Caramelised Onions
   120g sliced brown onions
   20g (1 tablespoon) caster sugar
   1 tablespoon white vinegar
   pinch of cracked black pepper
   pinch of salt
   1 teaspoon butter
   1 teaspoon olive oil
   pinch of thyme

Place all ingredients in a stainless steel pot and
bring to the boil. Cook, stirring often, reducing
until lightly caramelised. (Caution: do not let it
stick or burn.)

Twice-baked Onion Soufflés
   20g butter, melted
   2 cups fresh breadcrumbs
   335ml milk
   1 onion, studded with 3–4 cloves
   a few white peppercorns
   40g butter
   55g plain flour
   4 egg yolks
   caramelised onion mixture (above)
   25g grated parmesan
   pinch each of salt, pepper and nutmeg
   5 egg whites
   pinch of salt
   juice of 1 lemon

Brush 6 coffee cups or individual moulds with
melted butter. Dust with fresh breadcrumbs to
coat. Bring the milk, onion and peppercorns to
the boil then strain.

Melt butter, add flour then cook, stirring constantly for a few minutes, without colouring.
Add strained milk and cook, stirring until
smooth and thick.

Stir in the egg yolks, one at a time, over gentle
heat. Remove from heat. Stir in caramelised
onion, parmesan, salt, pepper and nutmeg.

Whisk egg whites in a mixer. Add a pinch of
salt and whisk for 30 seconds on low speed,
then on higher speed, adding lemon juice, until
whites are thick and firm.

Gradually (in 3–4 parts), fold beaten whites
into the onion sauce base.

Place soufflé mixture into prepared moulds.
Stand moulds in a water bath half full of luke-
warm water. Place on low shelf in preheated
oven at 170°C. Bake for 40–45 minutes. Let
cool slightly before removing from moulds.

Cracked Black Pepper Reduction
   40ml (2 tablespoons) oil
   beef trimmings
   6 shallots, peeled, chopped
   2 cloves garlic, peeled, chopped
   1 sprig rosemary
   100ml red wine
   400ml beef stock
   1 tablespoon arrowroot mixed with a little wine
   1 teaspoon cracked black peppercorns
   1/2 teaspoon Dijon mustard (optional)
   salt to taste

Heat oil in a saucepan and fry beef trimmings
until golden. Add shallots, garlic and rosemary.
Cook for 1 minute, stirring. Add wine and
reduce until almost all evaporated. Add stock,
bring to the boil, skim and simmer. Add
arrowroot mixture, stirring. Return to a boil,
strain and add cracked black pepper and mustard
if using. Season to taste.

The Beef
   6 beef fillet steaks, each 250g
   50ml olive oil
   salt and 1/4 teaspoon cracked black pepper

Heat a char-grill or grill-pan. Oil and season
the beef. Sear beef and cook to your liking.

To assemble: reheat soufflés on an oiled tray in
the oven for 5 minutes.

Warm 6 plates. Arrange blanched, glazed
spring vegetables on each plate with fillet steak,
a soufflé and a pool of sauce.

Serves 6

WINE

All Saints 1998 Shiraz
Estate grown in Rutherglen,
this classic regional Shiraz has
a richly flavoured varietal palate,
enhanced by sweet vanillin
American oak characters
and soft tannins. This is the
perfect wine to match the
rich flavours of the fillet and
its caramelised onions and
black pepper reduction.

RECIPE PREPARED BY
PETER WEIR
THE TERRACE RESTAURANT
ALL SAINTS ESTATE

*A classic Australian scene overlooking
All Saints' vineyard.*

Hume Weir Smoked Trout Risotto Dumplings

1 red onion, peeled, diced

2 cloves garlic, crushed

2 tablespoons olive oil

1 tablespoon butter

330g risotto (arborio) rice

1–1.2 litres boiling chicken stock

1 smoked trout, 300–500g, skinned, boned

50g grated parmesan

juice of 1 lemon

3 tablespoons chopped flat-leaf parsley

salt and pepper

coating: flour, beaten egg and dry breadcrumbs

oil for deep frying

Sauté onion and garlic in oil and butter over moderate heat until transparent.

Add rice and stir until coated. Reduce heat to low. Add 250ml of stock and stir briefly. Allow stock to absorb before adding another 250ml. Continue adding stock, stirring frequently until rice is almost cooked. Add flaked trout, parmesan, lemon juice, parsley and seasoning to taste. Pour into a dish to cool; stir occasionally.

When cold, roll rice into golf ball-size dumplings. (Or mould into flat patties.) Coat with flour, then egg and breadcrumbs.

RECIPE PREPARED BY
ALI MCKILLOP
THE PICKLED SISTERS CAFÉ
COFIELD WINES

Caper Salsa

1/2 cup capers, roughly chopped

1 bunch flat-leaf parsley, chopped

1/2 bunch chives, cut into batons

juice of 1 lemon

1 red onion, finely chopped

2 tablespoons extra virgin olive oil

salt and pepper

Mix all ingredients. Store in the fridge and use fresh on the day.

Horseradish Mustard Cream

1 cup sour cream

2 tablespoons Milawa Horseradish Seeded Mustard

salt and pepper

Combine all ingredients and season to taste.

To assemble: deep-fry risotto dumplings (or shallow fry patties) in hot oil. Drain and serve with Caper Salsa and Horseradish Mustard Cream. The chef adds a garnish of snow pea tendrils and a drizzle of turmeric oil.

Serves 4–6

Kicking back in a typical Australian country pub is part of the fun of travelling. The Rutherglen Hotel is just one of the historic hotels left over from a bustling era of gold mining and kept alive by wine industry success. The proprietor will not only welcome you with a cold beer and an affordable meal — he'll usually give you the insight into the best local attractions.

113

Risotto with Thyme and Fillets of Goulburn River Trout

Risotto

125g butter
3 cups risotto (arborio) rice
125ml Blackwood Park Riesling
3 litres hot chicken stock

Trout

6 fillets Goulburn River trout
seasoned flour
2 tablespoons fresh thyme leaves
shaved parmesan
thyme sprigs to garnish

Risotto: melt 25g of the butter in a large pot, add rice and stir to coat with butter.

Add the Riesling and let it evaporate. Stir in the stock, a cup at a time, until rice is cooked and stock absorbed.

Trout: coat trout fillets in seasoned flour. Pan-fry the fillets in remaining butter with thyme leaves.

To serve: place risotto on each plate and arrange trout fillets on top. Add shaved parmesan. Garnish with thyme sprigs.

Serves 6

WINE

Mitchelton 2000 Blackwood Park Riesling

Among Victoria's best Rieslings, this award-winning wine has a lovely floral aroma with hints of lemon blossom, and a touch of spice and marmalade. It has a perfectly balanced, mouth-filling palate and is delicious now, but with time the acid and fruit sweetness will build great complexity.

RECIPE PREPARED BY
BERNARD HAYES
MITCHELTON WINE BAR RESTAURANT
MITCHELTON WINES, GOULBURN VALLEY

Quintessential Australia — barren, sweeping paddocks, dotted gum trees parting at occasionally tumbling waterways — on the road from Rutherglen to Mitchelton Wines, a beautiful tourist discovery at Nagambie on the Goulburn River.

Antipasti

MADE FROM A WONDERFUL SELECTION OF
LOCAL PRODUCE

PREPARED BY
TRACY CHARLTON
BLUE PYRENEES ESTATE, AVOCA

Established nearly 40 years ago, this French-owned winery was known as Chateau Remy until 1996, when it became Blue Pyrenees to reflect the stunning mountain range which edges the vineyards. The French influence in winemaking has always driven sparkling wine production, but in recent years the winery has established a reputation for elegant red table wines, a more successful direction which it seems destined to follow.

WINE

Blue Pyrenees Estate Midnight Cuvee

The midnight grape pickers wear miners' helmets to find the Chardonnay and Pinot Noir bunches which go to make this wine. Night picking certainly assures optimum fruit quality and temperature control, resulting in this stylish wine with its lemon flavours and minerally length, ideal for a fresh antipasto.

Ararat

Ararat is a proud western Victorian rural stronghold, rich in its gold mining and pastoral history. While the small city offers an interesting range of architecture – from the 19th century Town Hall to this art deco hotel – it is primarily a wine tourist's stepping off point on the way to Avoca and the Pyrenees wine region, noted for its cool climate sparkling wines and elegant, ultra-premium reds.

Mount Avoca is one of the oldest vineyards in the region, with an impressive line-up of wines in an attractive setting.

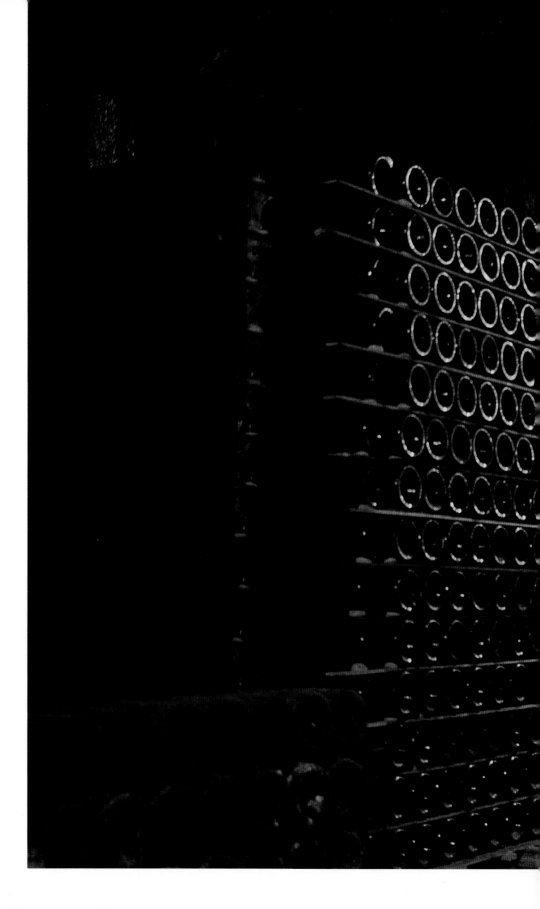

Seppelts Great Western

The cool, cobweb-lined labyrinth of tunnels under Seppelt Great
Western's winery and sparkling wine cellars was dug by gold
miners in the region in the 1860s. Now, the 2.5 kilometre
network of cellars and caves is used to store millions of bottles
of sparkling wine at a constant, perfect temperature.

A long, linear oasis. The wide, slow waters of the Murray are home to a wonderful range of bird and plant life, in marked contrast to the dry, brown lands of rural Australia through which it passes.

Mildura and the Murray River

Rolling lazily along for endless kilometres, the mighty Murray River is a vital artery to the many vignerons of the Riverland region. Without water from here, the millions of tonnes of grapes that form the backbone of the Australian wine industry simply could not be grown.

Most people have drunk the big-name wine brands that start life here, yet relatively few realise this is where they come from or that here is another worthy wine tourism region.

Not only wine grapes are grown near the banks of the Murray; the Riverland is also home to acres of Australian oranges, lemons, grapefruit and limes; avocados, peaches and plums. And the river itself is a world of its own, with peace, pelicans and a slow, easy pace.

Exotic palms and ferns near Mildura.

New South Wales

Vines arrived in Australia's most populous state when the First Fleet dropped anchor in 1788, but it wasn't until the 1830s that they were planted in the state's – and possibly Australia's – best known wine region, the Hunter Valley. Its relative proximity to Sydney, about three hours' drive north, has ensured that wine tourism has boomed, and more visitors tread a path to the Lower and Upper Hunter than any other region.

There is, as you'd expect, much to see and enjoy up here, with fine restaurants, stylish resorts and, of course, plenty of the region's wines – most notably, leathery, earthy Shiraz and remarkable Semillon, which starts lean and tart when young, but with age – and no help from oak maturation – acquires a toasty lanolin complexity you'd swear came from a barrel.

Of course, there's far more to New South Wales than the Hunter – up in the hills, Mudgee is producing increasing quantities of fine reds, while down in the vast irrigated plains of Riverina, the most luscious dessert wines are made (and Italian immigrant heritage means there is some fantastic food to be found in unlikely places).

There are newer regions, too, up in the cooler, high-altitude climes of the more southerly hills at Orange, Hilltops, Tumbarumba and Canberra District. Though the climate is challenging, all are now home to increasing numbers of high-quality wines, with great whites and some promising reds; the attendant cellar doors and restaurants are starting to follow.

But most people's visits to New South Wales will start and end in Sydney, and if you're not too fussed about seeking out scenery and driving, well, why not? All the wines you could wish to try are sold here and, more to the point, the city still has one of the most exciting food scenes in the world. Eclectic, inspired cuisine is commonplace, the harbourside setting unparalleled. Other regions may have more charm or offer better value, but if you have a love for living as well as fine wine and food, Sydney can't be bettered.

The wide open spaces of pasture and vineyard at Len Evans' Tower Estate in the Lower Hunter.

Trifle of Mascarpone, Berries and Champagne Jelly

Almond Sponge
    100g flour
    75g almond meal (ground almonds)
    75g icing sugar
    300g eggs (about 5)
    95g sugar
    1 tablespoon glucose
    seeds from 1/2 vanilla pod
    65g butter, melted

Sift together flour, almond meal and icing sugar.

Whisk eggs, sugar, glucose and vanilla pod seeds in a bowl over a pot of simmering water until the mixture reaches 50°C (warm, not hot to your finger). Continue to whisk off the heat until the mixture leaves smooth ribbons when you lift the whisk.

Mix 1/3 of the egg into the melted butter until combined. Fold the flour mixture into the remaining egg until combined. Then fold the butter/egg mixture into the flour/egg mixture until combined.

Spread the batter in a 22cm diameter baking tin, base-lined with paper, sides buttered and floured. Bake at 180°C for about 30 minutes.

Berry Marmalade
    2 punnets strawberries
    1 punnet each raspberries, boysenberries
    1/2 cup sugar
    1 1/2 teaspoons pectin powder (e.g. Jamsetta)
    1/2 vanilla pod
    zest and juice of 1/2 lime
    1 punnet each blackberries, blueberries

Slice 1 1/2 punnets of strawberries. Add 1/2 punnet raspberries and 1/2 punnet boysenberries.

Mix sugar, pectin and split vanilla pod then gently toss with sliced strawberry mixture. Add lime zest and juice. Set aside for 10 minutes.

Combine remaining berries, dicing the 1/2 punnet of strawberries. Set aside.

Put the berry-sugar mix into a pan and cook over gentle heat for 5 minutes to dissolve sugar and release berry juices. Increase heat to medium and cook for 5 more minutes.

Remove from heat, cool to room temperature then gently combine with remaining berries.

Mascarpone Cream
    500g mascarpone
    2 eggs, separated
    60g sugar

Whisk mascarpone, egg yolks and 1/2 the sugar until stiff. Whisk egg whites and remaining sugar to stiff peaks. Fold whites into mascarpone.

Champagne Jelly
    4 leaves gelatine
        (or 2 teaspoons powdered gelatine)
    375ml Croser Sparkling or Champagne
    375ml sugar syrup (1/2 sugar, 1/2 water)
    extra sparkling wine to moisten sponge

Soak gelatine in a little of the wine until soft. Heat sugar syrup to just below simmering, add softened gelatine and stir to dissolve.

Add remaining wine and pour into a container so the jelly is 1.5–2cm deep. Refrigerate to set.

To assemble: trim crusts off sponge. Place sponge in serving bowls. Spoon some extra champagne over the sponge to moisten. Spoon the Berry Marmalade on to the sponge. Cover berries with Mascarpone Cream. Dice jelly in the container. Tumble jelly cubes over the mascarpone. Garnish each with 2–3 berries if you like.

Serves 6

RECIPE PREPARED BY
CATHERINE ADAMS
ROCKPOOL, SYDNEY

WINE

Petaluma 1998 Croser
Rockpool is one of the cornerstones of Sydney's fashionable restaurants, and its Champagne jelly trifle is a thrillingly decadent testimony as to why. Try the classic Croser with it and you'll find a tight, clean, delicate sparkler with great structure and length. Cuts through the marscapone cream like a knife.

Ballotine of Ocean Trout

1 ocean trout fillet, 1.5kg (1/2 whole fish)
salt and a pinch cayenne pepper
1/4 cup each chopped Italian parsley and dill
1/4 cup each chopped chervil and chives

Lemon Vinaigrette
50ml lemon juice
250ml extra virgin olive oil

Acidulated Cream
200ml double cream
15ml (3 teaspoons) lemon juice
1/2 bunch dill, chopped
salt and pepper

To serve
1 cucumber, peeled, thinly sliced,
    seeds removed
1 bunch chives, chopped
salt and pepper
250g spanner crab white meat, picked
100g ocean trout roe
2 serrano chillies, diced
1 bunch land cress, about 50g

Cut ocean trout fillet lengthwise, removing the thinner belly, to leave an even cylindrical shape. Season with salt and cayenne. Mix the chopped herbs together and cover the fish, pressing down firmly.

Tightly roll the fish in a large piece of cling-wrap. Tie at each end to form a ballotine. (This must be watertight.)

Place fish into a wide pan of water at 65°C (use a thermometer), submerge the fish and cook for 2 minutes, maintaining the temperature at 65°C. Remove pan from the heat, leaving the ballotine to cool in the water. When cool, refrigerate ballotine overnight.

Lemon Vinaigrette: whisk ingredients together.

Acidulated Cream: whip cream and mix in lemon juice, chopped dill, salt and pepper.

To assemble: slice the ballotine (cling-wrap still on), into rounds, about 120g each.

Mix cucumber and chives with a small amount of lemon vinaigrette, salt and pepper.

Mix crab meat with a little ocean trout roe, diced chillies, chopped chives, lemon vinaigrette, salt and pepper.

To serve: place cucumber mixture on the centre of each plate. Place crab mixture on top of the cucumber. Arrange ocean trout (cling-wrap removed) on the crab meat. Top with a little ocean trout roe.

Decorate each plate with land cress and a quenelle of acidulated cream, then drizzle lemon vinaigrette around.

Serves 10

RECIPE PREPARED BY
PETER DOYLE
CELSIUS RESTAURANT, SYDNEY

WINE

Delatite 1999 Riesling
Celsius is Peter Doyle's latest culinary venture and it has something of an upbeat, retro, Sydney 2000 feel about it. This delicate Delatite Riesling was recommended with the Ocean Trout Ballotine, and its combination of a floral, spicy bouquet and a crisp, fresh finish certainly suits it well.

A fountain at the end of King's Cross, Sydney's infamous red light district. There's more to see than sleaze, however, and as a result of the 2000 Olympics, accommodation, roads and services have been improved dramatically.

A sunlit Sydney skyline.

Angel Hair Pasta

WITH TUNA, CHILLI AND ROCKET

250g angel hair pasta
juice of 1 lemon
100ml extra virgin olive oil
50ml chilli oil*
1 clove garlic, crushed
salt and ground black pepper
200g sashimi tuna, thinly sliced
4 basil leaves, shredded
100g parmesan cheese, grated
4 teaspoons salted capers, washed
1 bunch rocket, chopped

Cook pasta in a large saucepan of salted, boiling water for 3 minutes or until al dente. Drain.

Combine lemon juice, olive oil, chilli oil, garlic, salt and pepper in a screw-top jar and shake well.

Place the tuna, basil, parmesan, capers and rocket in a large bowl. Drizzle over the dressing and toss gently. Add drained pasta to tuna mixture, toss gently to combine then serve.

This can be prepared and served in less than 30 minutes.

Serves 4 as an entrée, 2 as a main course.

To make Chilli Oil: remove seeds from 6 small red chillies. Finely chop chillies. Place chillies and 250ml olive oil in a saucepan over low heat until the oil becomes clear. Allow to cool, strain, then store in an air-tight jar.

RECIPE PREPARED BY
ANDY DAVIES
DARLING MILLS RESTAURANT, SYDNEY

WINE

Tyrrells 1992 Vat 1 Semillon

This classic Hunter Semillon, aged before release, reeks of lemon and butter. It will continue to develop further for years to come, but for now it is perfect with the textures and flavours of this Angel Hair Pasta.

Warm Salad of Barbecued Scallops and Prawns

ON GLASS NOODLES WITH TURMERIC DRESSING

Seafood

8 green prawns, peeled, de-veined
8 fresh scallops, roe removed
1 teaspoon ground turmeric
1/2 teaspoon salt
1/2 teaspoon pepper
2 tablespoons sunflower oil

Combine turmeric, salt, pepper and oil and toss with seafood. Marinate for 30 minutes.

Salad

1 bunch asparagus
1 red capsicum
1/2 packet glass noodles (bean thread or
   cellophane noodles)
1 cup mesclun salad mix

Cook and refresh asparagus.
Char-grill capsicum. Place capsicum in a plastic bag to sweat for 15 minutes, then clean out seeds and peel off skin. Cut flesh into julienne.
Pour boiling water over the noodles and let stand for 3-4 minutes. Rinse in cold water then drain.

Dressing

1 teaspoon ground turmeric
1 teaspoon ground cumin
pinch each of salt, pepper and cayenne
2 tablespoons olive oil
1 tablespoon lemon juice

Combine all ingredients.

To assemble: drain oil marinade off seafood. Lightly smear a skillet with marinating oil and bring to high heat. Sear prawns on both sides until done (about 2 minutes). Remove.
Add scallops to the pan and sear for 30 seconds on each side. Remove.
Arrange a mound of glass noodles on each plate and drizzle with a teaspoon of dressing. Arrange mesclun on top of noodles. Stack asparagus and capsicum strips against the noodles and drizzle with a teaspoon of dressing. Place the prawns and scallops around the mesclun and drizzle remaining dressing over the seafood.

Serves 2

Intricate carvings of sinuous vines adorn this doorway at Mount Pleasant Wines.

RECIPE PREPARED BY
CLIFF KILNER
ELIZABETH'S CAFÉ
MOUNT PLEASANT WINES, HUNTER VALLEY

WINE

Mount Pleasant 1999 Verdelho
This Portuguese grape variety appears well suited to the soils and climate of the Hunter Valley if this Mount Pleasant example is anything to go by. There are exotic and tropical fruit nuances on nose and palate, but the structure is firm with clean acidity. Wonderful with shellfish.

Warm King Prawn, Baby Beetroot, Roast Carrot and Rocket Salad

RECIPE PREPARED BY
MARK HOSIE
THE CELLAR RESTAURANT
HUNTER VALLEY

WITH CARDAMOM AND ORANGE DRESSING

Vegetables

    20 baby beetroot
    1 tablespoon olive oil
    2 carrots
    1 tablespoon brown sugar
    1/2 tablespoon balsamic vinegar
    100g rocket
    12 cherry tomatoes

Roast baby beetroot in their skins with the olive oil until tender. Peel the carrots and cut into four. Dust carrots with brown sugar and roast at 200°C until just tender.
Deglaze the pan with balsamic vinegar.

Dressing

    3 oranges
    6 cardamom pods, lightly crushed
    1 tablespoon caster sugar
    1 tablespoon white vinegar
    300ml olive oil
    salt and pepper

Combine zest of 1 orange and the juice of 3 oranges with cardamom, sugar and vinegar. Bring to the boil then simmer until the liquid is reduced by half. Strain and while warm whisk in the oil and season.

Prawns

    20 green prawns, peeled and de-veined
    1 teaspoon sea salt
    1 teaspoon each ground cumin and paprika
    1 1/4 teaspoons ground black pepper
    1 tablespoon flour
    2 tablespoons vegetable oil for cooking

Mix dry ingredients and lightly dust over prawns. In a heavy-based pan heat vegetable oil until nearly smoking. Add prawns and cook until just firm. Remove from the pan.

To assemble: lightly dress the rocket and arrange on plates with beetroot, cherry tomatoes and carrots on top. Then add prawns and drizzle the dressing around the outside of the stack.

Serves 4

Uncleared bushland, left, near Ian and Jan Savage's Cellar Restaurant.

Grilled Lobster Tail

WITH MUSSELS AND SEARED SCALLOPS
AND GINGER AND SOBA NOODLE SALAD

Seafood

   2 lobster tails, halved
   salt and pepper
   8 fresh mussels
   8–12 scallops, roe on
   20g clarified butter or ghee
   watercress to garnish

Noodles

   200g soba (buckwheat) noodles
   40g pickled ginger
   40ml (2 tablespoons) sesame oil

Vinaigrette

   6 ripe tomatoes, chopped
   1/2 bunch tarragon, chopped
   1/2 bunch basil, chopped
   1/2 teaspoon cayenne pepper
   1/2 teaspoon sugar
   500ml extra virgin olive oil

Grill lobster tails then season. Steam open mussels.

Soba Noodle Salad: cook noodles in boiling, salted water until just tender. Drain and cool. Combine ginger and sesame oil and mix with cold noodles.

Vinaigrette: place all ingredients in a metal bowl. Warm slowly to infuse. Press through a sieve using a large spoon. Cool, then refrigerate.

To assemble: sear scallops in clarified butter in a hot pan for 1 minute on each side.

Place noodles on 4 plates with 1/2 lobster tail on top of each. Arrange scallops and mussels in the half shell around the noodles and add vinaigrette. Garnish with watercress.

Serves 4

RECIPE PREPARED BY
HARRY CALLINAN
ROBERTS AT PEPPER TREE, HUNTER VALLEY

Beautiful gardens and immaculate vineyards surround Pepper Tree Wines, where you can enjoy the inspired cooking of Robert Molines as well as fine Hunter wines.

Warm Salad of Fresh Asparagus

WITH RILEY'S FROMAGE BLANC AND BASIL
AND BALSAMIC BRAISED ROMAS

Braised Roma Tomatoes

6 ripe roma tomatoes, blanched, skins removed
1 small onion, finely diced
1/2 clove garlic, peeled, finely chopped
1 tablespoon olive oil
1/2 bunch basil, leaves only, finely sliced
2 teaspoons balsamic vinegar
1 tablespoon white wine
salt and pepper

Place tomatoes in an oven-proof, ceramic dish. Sauté onion and garlic in a little of the oil until clear. Sprinkle this over tomatoes with remaining ingredients. Cover and cook in the oven at 180°C for about 15 minutes. Remove from the oven, turn tomatoes over, re-cover, then cook for 15 more minutes. Tomatoes should be still firm enough to handle. Allow to cool in the juices then slice in half lengthwise.

Balsamic and Mustard Dressing

100ml good balsamic vinegar
200ml olive oil
30ml medium sherry
1 rounded teaspoon wholeseed mustard
1 rounded teaspoon honey
sea salt and pepper to taste

Whisk together and adjust seasoning.

Salad

100g rocket (preferably wild)
500g Riley's Fromage Blanc*

24 spears fresh asparagus
   (even thickness, under 1cm diameter)
4 thin slices prosciutto, grilled until crisp
shreds of roasted red pepper to garnish
freshly ground black pepper

To assemble: remove any thick, bitter stems from rocket. Toss rocket in a little Balsamic Mustard Dressing (left-over dressing keeps well). Place a small mound of rocket on each plate. Top with 3 tomato halves. Pour some of their juices around the rocket.

Using two dessertspoons, mould 3 quenelles of the cheese for each plate. Place outside the rocket.

If asparagus spears are thick, shave ends with a potato peeler. Blanch asparagus in boiling water for about 1 minute until tender. Place asparagus over tomatoes and rocket.

Break prosciutto into shards; scatter over plates. Garnish with shreds of roasted red pepper. Grind over some black pepper. Serve with crusty bread.

Serves 4

*For Riley's Fromage Blanc (Hunter Valley Cheese Company) substitute a fresh, soft cream cheese, or fresh curd cheese such as fromage frais.

RECIPE PREPARED BY
JULIE VAN DEN BERG
CAFÉ CROCODILE, WANDIN VALLEY ESTATE
HUNTER VALLEY

WINE

*Wandin Valley
WVE Reserve Chardonnay
Geoff Broadfield's Chardonnay has lovely nutty characters with peach fruit flavours and a smooth, buttery finish. It goes well with the warm asparagus salad made by Julie Van Den Berg at the winery's Café Crocodile.*

Wandin Valley Estate sits in classic Hunter territory of gums and vineyards, with the shelf of the Broken Back Range in the background.

The lake at Capercaillie looking back towards the winery buildings. Platters of local cheese and fruit are sold at the cellar door.

Cheese and Fruit Platter

PLATTER PREPARED BY
CAPERCAILLIE WINE COMPANY
HUNTER VALLEY

WINE

Capercaillie Shiraz

A typically full and generous Shiraz made from top quality Hunter fruit by the genial Alasdair Sutherland.
Powerful upfront fruit with earthy overtones and great depth and structure. More than a match for a cheese platter.

There's a distinctly Mediterranean feel to the Tower Estate winery and Tower Lodge accommodation.

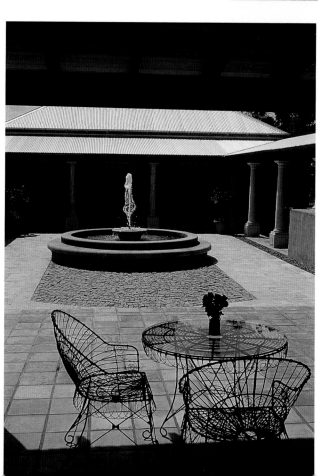

The Lower Hunter Valley

With its easy access to Sydney weekenders, the Lower Hunter has long been ahead of the game when it comes to wine tourist facilities at all levels. The more discerning traveller now has an added incentive to visit, with Len Evans' creation of the luxurious Tower Lodge.

Antique furniture and works of art, fine linen, individually designed rooms and food by Robert Molines add up to the most indulgent of escapes.

Vines at Brokenwood, producer of some of the Hunter's finest wines.

Fermentation tanks at Rosemount provide a stark contrast to the rows of vines and hills and escarpments of the Upper Hunter.

Rosemount

Far less crowded and with fewer wineries, the Upper Hunter Valley is something of an oasis compared with some of the busier tourist routes of the Hunter region. The area is dominated by Rosemount, the dynamic family wine company that recently merged with wine industry colossus Southcorp. The winery and restaurant at Denman is set on a slope overlooking the meandering Gouldburn River, and is a pleasant place to spend a while.

Thriving young vines in the Hunter.

Rosemount enjoys wonderful views from its Upper Hunter winery and vineyards.

The wide open spaces and big blue skies provide some wonderful panoramas in the country between the Hunter Valley and Mudgee.

Plump, healthy grapes ready to yield their precious juice.

147

Herbed Feta with Eggplant

AND PINE NUT HONEY DRESSING

1 eggplant (aubergine)

300g feta cheese, grated

80g ricotta cheese

2 tablespoons chopped fresh herbs
  (e.g. dill, oregano)

oil

3 red capsicums, roasted, skinned, seeds
  removed

Dressing

  50g currants

  50g pine nuts, toasted

  1 clove garlic, crushed

  1/4 cup each red wine vinegar, olive oil

  1 tablespoon honey

  salt and pepper

  finely chopped parsley

Thinly slice the eggplant then char-grill.
Mix the cheeses and herbs.

Oil six (1 cup capacity) ramekins. Line the bottom of ramekins with eggplant. Add a layer of capsicum, then some cheese mixture. Repeat layers, finishing with eggplant. Chill for 1–2 hours until set.

Dressing: whisk all ingredients together.

To serve: run a blunt knife around the sides of the ramekins. Invert each ramekin on to a plate and un-mould. Drizzle the mounds with dressing.

Serves 6

The winery at Craigmoor is the oldest in the region and its restaurant one of the most popular. The terrace overlooking the perfectly manicured cricket pitch is an ideal spot for a leisurely lunch.

RECIPE PREPARED BY
RUSSELL MARCHENKO
CRAIGMOOR RESTAURANT
POET'S CORNER WINERY, MUDGEE

WINE

*Poet's Corner 2000 Henry Lawson
Semillon*

Spritzy and leaping with lemon freshness, this Henry Lawson Semillon cuts a dash with the herbed feta dish served at Craigmoor. Delicious now, but with the backbone to age and develop for a good 10 years.

Cutlet of Veal

WITH MUSHROOM FRITTATA,
SAUTÉ CHERRY TOMATOES WITH GARLIC AND BASIL,
AND A CABERNET JUS

6 veal cutlets, frenched, each 200g

Frittata
250g assorted mushrooms, sliced
2 cloves garlic, peeled, finely chopped
80g butter
9 eggs

2 punnets ripe cherry tomatoes
1/2 bunch basil, shredded
50ml olive oil
salt and pepper
300ml good quality cabernet jus

Frittata: sauté mushrooms and garlic in the butter. Drain off excess water.

Lightly whisk eggs. Mix in mushrooms and garlic.

Cook in small blini pans, or make one large frittata in a fry-pan; heat a little oil in the pan, add egg mixture to almost fill. Cook gently on stove top for a few minutes, then complete cooking in a moderate oven until firm. Turn out and keep warm. Cut into desired shapes.

Char-grill the veal cutlets to your liking, rest and keep warm.

Sweeping views from the award-winning winery, restaurant and function complex at Highland Heritage Estate in Orange, which is popular with locals and visitors alike.

WINE

*Highland Heritage Estate 1997
Mount Canobolas Chardonnay*

A classic example of cool climate Chardonnay, with lifted floral and peach aromas backed by soft, creamy oak. In the mouth, it is full-bodied, yet finishes dry and crisp — a good partner for Paul Wilderbeek's veal and mushroom frittata dish.

Sauté cherry tomatoes and shredded basil in olive oil until tomatoes soften slightly. Season well.

Heat jus.

To serve: place tomato/basil mixture on each plate. Arrange mushroom frittata on top. Add cutlets and jus to finish.

Serves 6

RECIPE PREPARED BY
PAUL WILDERBEEK
HIGHLAND HERITAGE ESTATE
MOUNT CANOBOLAS

Warm Asian Salad of Cowra Lamb

2 racks of lamb (4 cutlets each), well trimmed
1 bunch green asparagus
mixed lettuce leaves
fresh coriander
semi-dried tomatoes
red onion, thinly sliced

Poaching Liquid
2 cups good quality beef stock
1/3 cup soy sauce
2 tablespoons sweet chilli sauce
1 tablespoon tomato paste
1 tablespoon chopped coriander
1 tablespoon chopped lemongrass
1 teaspoon grated ginger
1 teaspoon crushed garlic

Bake lamb racks in a hot oven for 15 minutes.
Combine all poaching liquid ingredients in a large skillet and bring to the boil. Stir until well combined. Reduce heat to a low simmer.
Cut the lamb into individual cutlets and gently poach for 10 minutes with the asparagus.

While lamb is poaching, make up 2 plates of mixed lettuce. Sprinkle with fresh coriander. Place drained asparagus and lamb on top of the salad and spoon poaching liquid over as a dressing. Garnish with semi-dried tomatoes and thinly sliced red onion.
Serve with good quality grilled Italian bread.

Serves 2

RECIPE PREPARED BY
PAUL LOVERIDGE
THE QUARRY RESTAURANT AND CELLARS
COWRA

WINE

Cowra Estate 1999 Cabernet Rosé
What better with a warm Asian salad of rare pink lamb in a summer garden setting than a refreshing pink wine like Cowra Estate's luscious, easy drinking Cabernet Rosé. A delicious, berry fruit-filled mouthful with a touch of spice, and decidedly more-ish.

The deep and shady verandahs at Paul Loveridge's Quarry Restaurant and Cellars are a perfect summer vantage point to view the beautiful gardens.

Melanzane Marinara

4 medium-sized eggplants

salt

olive oil

400g green prawns

pepper and salt

2 cloves garlic, peeled, roughly chopped

1 roasted red capsicum, peeled, de-seeded

1 small bunch basil

flour for dusting

6 eggs, lightly beaten

1kg fresh breadcrumbs from Italian-style bread

1 cup flat-leaf parsley, chopped

2 teaspoons dried oregano

mixed salad and lemon wedges to serve

Peel and slice eggplants into rounds about 6mm thick. Sprinkle with salt and leave to disgorge for about 30 minutes. Pat eggplant dry. Fry in a little olive oil until coloured but still firm. Drain on absorbent paper.

Peel and de-vein prawns. Cook prawns in a little olive oil in a non-stick pan, adding salt, pepper and chopped garlic, until about 3/4 cooked (do not over-cook).

Put prawns, roasted capsicum and basil into a processor and pulse to the texture of coarse breadcrumbs. Set aside.

Make eggplant slices into sandwiches, filling them with the prawn mixture. Dust with flour, coat in the beaten egg, then coat with breadcrumbs and the herbs.

Shallow fry in hot olive oil. Drain and serve with mixed salad and lemon wedges.

Serves 4

RECIPE PREPARED BY
SAM VICO
BASSANO CAFÉ, GRIFFITH

WINE

Riverina Wines 1164 Chairman's Selection Semillon
A luscious, lemony Semillon that is clean and refreshing but has enough body and weight to stand up wonderfully to the rich seafood sandwiches served at Griffith's Bassano Café. A perfect combination.

Olive trees and an ornamental gateway form part of the pretty gardens surrounding De Bortoli's Riverina winery near Griffith, home of one of Australia's finest dessert wines, Noble One Botrytis Semillon.

Western Australia

Sitting in truly splendid isolation on the very edge of a vast continent, Western Australia really is an awfully long way away from anywhere else. There are wide expanses of desert on one side and the Indian Ocean on the other, so the sparkling city of Perth and the gem of a wine region that is Margaret River, three hours south, come as unexpected delights, true oases, especially for lovers of fine food and wine.

This is a young wine state and decidedly small-scale compared to the veritable stalwarts of South Australia and Victoria. Vines have only been planted in Margaret River since the mid-1960s, and there is still a sense of promise and enthusiasm that there are discoveries yet to be made.

It might not look like classic wine country, with its dairy farms, karri gum forests and wild, rolling surf beaches, but the patches of vines here certainly produce classic wines – Cabernet Sauvignon with a nod to Bordeaux, Chardonnay in the Burgundian mould and sublime blends of Sauvignon Blanc and Semillon. Warm summers tempered by the ever-present ocean influence rein in the ripe, full flavours for which Australian wines are so well known, held in check with elegance, balance and finesse.

Wineries are diverse – sometimes cute, sometimes startling; rustic on one side of the road, state of the art on the other – and a shopping paradise for oenophiles, with sophisticated selections of glasses, gadgetry, clothing and paraphernalia on sale along with the wines. Ultra-smart eateries are plentiful, too, usually attached to wineries in sylvan settings, with the abundant local seafood, shellfish, meat and dairy produce deftly handled in a number of styles.

Even more culinary delights are to be found in the capital, a clean, bright, easy-going place with an air of good living and well-being. Whether in the narrow streets of the historic city centre or in a sleek waterfront setting, Perth abounds in great restaurants serving fine, modern food. Bright sunshine, blue water, fresh food and fine wine – a great place to escape to!

Local reef shark from the spectacular rocky surf beaches just minutes from Cullen Wines in Cowramup, home of superb wines from the mother and daughter team of Di and Vanya Cullen.

Poisson Cru of Local Reef Shark

WITH GLASS NOODLE SALAD

Poisson Cru
    500g fresh bronze whaler shark fillets*
    juice of 3 limes
    500ml fish sauce (nam pla)
    5ml (1 teaspoon) chilli oil

Salad
    50g glass noodles
        (cellophane/bean thread noodles)
    50g snow pea sprouts
    1/2 carrot, cut into julienne
    coriander sprigs
    thumb-size knob of fresh ginger, peeled,
        cut in fine julienne
    2 cloves garlic, peeled, cut in fine julienne
    1 fresh chilli, de-seeded, finely diced
    1 1/2 spring onions, sliced
    sprinkle of fried garlic slices**

Dressing
    zest and juice of 1 lime
    2 teaspoons fish sauce
    1 tablespoon olive oil
    salt and pepper
    1 drop sesame oil

Poisson Cru: cut fish into very fine slices. Brush liberally with mix of lime juice, fish sauce and chilli oil. Cover and marinate in the refrigerator for 12 hours.

Salad: soak noodles in hot water for 3–4 minutes. Rinse with cold water. Drain. Mix with all salad ingredients. Whisk together dressing ingredients. Toss with salad.

To assemble: arrange fish around the plates, salad in the centre. Drizzle fish with chilli oil. The chef adds a finishing touch of Malaysian dark, caramel soy sauce (Cheong Chan), 3 spots on each plate. Serve cold and fresh.

Serves 4

*Substitute gummy shark, or dhufish (West Australian jewfish).
**Peeled, sliced garlic, deep-fried in oil until golden. Available ready-prepared from Thai or Asian food stockists.

RECIPES PREPARED BY
HAMISH MCLEAY
CULLEN DINING
CULLEN WINES, MARGARET RIVER

Seared Swordfish on Parsnip Mash

WITH ASIAN COLESLAW, BROAD BEANS AND
FRIED CHILLI SAMBAL

Asian Coleslaw
    250g Chinese cabbage, finely shredded
    a little chopped chilli, garlic and fresh ginger
    1 carrot, cut in julienne
    2 spring onions, sliced
    coriander leaves, picked
    6 leaves Vietnamese mint, finely chopped

Dressing
    1 teaspoon wasabi paste
    50ml each lime juice and light soy sauce
    1 drop sesame oil
    salt and pepper

Combine coleslaw ingredients and toss with dressing ingredients.

Broad Beans
    1 1/2 cups frozen broad beans (or fresh, podded)
    extra virgin olive oil, black pepper

Blanch or cook beans. Refresh, drain, then peel. Toss with oil and pepper.

Fried Chilli Sambal
Slowly heat 100g each of chopped fresh chilli, ginger and garlic in olive oil until garlic lightly browns. Remove from heat. Cool, then blitz in a food processor. Strain (keep oil for chilli oil).

Parsnip Mash
    3 potatoes, peeled
    3 parsnips, peeled
    100ml cream
    60g butter
    salt and pepper
    fried parsnip chips to garnish (optional)

Boil potatoes and parsnips until soft. Drain, add cream and butter, then mash. Season.

Seared Swordfish
    4–8 swordfish steaks, each 1.5cm thick
    salt, pepper and oil

In a very hot, oiled pan, sear seasoned fish until medium-rare (do not over-cook).

To serve: arrange 1 or 2 fish steaks on each plate with hot mash, salad, sambal and broad beans. Garnish with parsnip chips if you like.

Serves 4

Cambinata Yabby Salad

12 yabbies (small fresh-water crayfish)*
1 stalk lemon grass
a few slices fresh ginger
1/2 cup red or green grapes
2 mignonette or loose-leaf lettuces,
    1 red, 1 green

Dressing
    1 tablespoon white palm sugar
        (or raw or caster sugar)
    zest and juice of 1 lemon
    zest and juice of 1 orange
    1 tablespoon sweet soy sauce
    2 tablespoons water
    1/2 red chilli, de-seeded, finely chopped
    2 tablespoons Brookland Valley verjuice
        (or available verjuice or lemon juice)
    4 tablespoons olive oil
    1 tablespoon chopped fresh coriander

Steam yabbies over water containing lemon grass and ginger for 5–7 minutes.
Peel the tails and crack the claws. Refrigerate.
Halve and de-seed grapes. Wash lettuces and dry well. Chill until required.

Dressing: Bring palm sugar, lemon and orange zest and juice, soy sauce and water just to the boil. Remove from heat. Add chopped chilli,

WINE
Brookland Valley 2000 Sauvignon Blanc
An intensely aromatic wine with tropical hints of passionfruit and white peach. Pungent gooseberry fruit flavours and a soft, herbaceous palate give a refreshing, racy wine with good length.

verjuice, olive oil and coriander. Mix well. (The dressing should be sweet and refreshing with a hint of chilli, coriander and grape flavours, and vibrant in colour from zests.)

To assemble: Place lettuce leaves and halved, de-seeded grapes in a bowl. Toss well with dressing. Arrange on plates with the yabbies. Serve chilled.

Serves 4

*The chef uses farmed yabbies from Cambinata, Western Australia but you can use other fresh crustaceans.

RECIPE PREPARED BY
ALFRED QUINTUS
FLUTES OF BROOKLAND VALLEY
BROOKLAND VALLEY WINES

Winding paths through green banks lined with lavender and cottage plants lead you through Brookland Valley Wines to the light and airy Flutes restaurant overlooking a lake and vineyards.

Chorizo and Sage Stuffed Chicken

ON TOMATO AND BASIL CONFIT WITH
ENGLISH SPINACH AND HUMMUS

Tomato and Basil Confit

>   20 roma tomatoes
>   1 cup olive oil
>   5 cloves garlic, peeled, sliced
>   1 can (425g) peeled tomatoes, drained
>   2 cups basil, chopped
>   1/2 ciabatta loaf, crust removed

Blanch, peel and chop tomatoes. In a heavy-based pan heat 1/2 cup of olive oil and sweat the sliced garlic until soft but not brown. Add the fresh and canned tomatoes (without juice). Cook until thick. Add chopped basil. Remove from heat. Dice the bread then stir in. Add the remaining 1/2 cup of oil.

Hummus

>   4 cups cooked, drained chick peas
>   2 tablespoons tahini
>   juice of 2 lemons
>   2 cloves garlic, peeled, crushed
>   1/2 cup olive oil
>   1/4 cup chopped parsley

Blend all ingredients together in a food processor until smooth.

Chicken

>   4 boneless chicken breasts, skin on
>   2 chorizo sausages
>   salt and pepper
>   fresh sage leaves, finely chopped
>   1 bunch English spinach
>   butter and olive oil
>   deep-fried basil leaves

Make a small incision in each chicken breast and push a 1/2 chorizo sausage into the cavity with seasoning and chopped sage.

Sear chicken breasts in a little hot oil in a frying pan. Then transfer to the oven at 180°C for 15 minutes. Remove and let rest in a warm place.

To serve: wilt the spinach in a little hot butter. Divide Tomato Confit between 4 deep plates. Place spinach on tomato. Slice the chicken on the diagonal, and arrange on top, twisting slices to get a little height. Add hummus, garnish with deep-fried basil and drizzle a little olive oil around.

RECIPE PREPARED BY
JASON LARSEN
LEEUWIN ESTATE

Set among towering karri gums and dramatic gardens, Leeuwin Estate is almost as well known for its winery restaurant and its annual concert under the stars as for its stellar range of premium wines.

WINE

Leeuwin Estate 1997 Art Series Chardonnay
Thought by many to be among Australia's finest wines, Leeuwin's Art Series Chardonnay is indeed a classic. The bouquet is a complex mélange of creamy fruit and butter aromas, the palate a rounded, full-bodied mouthful of fine fruit and French oak, perfectly balanced.

Harissa Lamb

WITH SPICED LENTILS, PUMPKIN PICKLE
AND TAHINI YOGHURT

4 lamb rumps, trimmed

Harissa Paste

2 teaspoons each ground cumin and coriander

2 teaspoons caraway seeds

100g red chillies

6 cloves garlic, peeled

2 tablespoons each chopped mint and coriander

juice of 1 lemon

olive oil as required

Process all ingredients to form a paste. Rub paste over lamb rumps. Marinate overnight.

Pumpkin Pickle

1 large butternut or small pumpkin

2–3 tablespoons olive oil

1 brown onion, peeled, diced

1 teaspoon caraway seeds

1 teaspoon garam masala

300ml each balsamic and white vinegar

300ml water

200g brown sugar

salt and pepper

Remove peel and seeds from butternut. Cut into cubes. Heat oil in a large, heavy-based saucepan. Add butternut, onion and spices. Sauté until brown. Add vinegars, water and brown sugar. Cook over low heat, stirring often, for about 1 hour, until butternut is soft. Add salt and pepper. Cool, cover and refrigerate.

Tahini Yoghurt: combine 200ml natural yoghurt, juice of 1 lemon and 2 teaspoons tahini.

Spiced Lentils

2 tablespoons olive oil

1 brown onion, peeled, chopped

50g crushed garlic

50g crushed red chillies

2 teaspoons each ground cumin and coriander

500g whole, peeled tomatoes

250g green puy lentils, soaked for 1 hour

salt and pepper

Place oil in a saucepan on high heat. Add onion, garlic, chillies, and spices and cook until onions are soft.

RECIPE PREPARED BY
AARON CARR
BALCONY RESTAURANT, VASSE FELIX
MARGARET RIVER

164

WINE

Vasse Felix 1999 Cabernet Sauvignon Another Margaret River classic this, with its complex nose of cranberry, plum and currant aromas, supported by earthy, hardwood notes from its oak maturation. The palate is rich and tight with sweet berry and plum flavours supported by fine tannins. Winemaker Clive Otto recommends this with Aaron Carr's spicy Harissa Lamb.

Add tomatoes and simmer gently.

Drain soaked lentils and add to 2 litres of boiling water. Simmer for about 40 minutes until cooked but not soft. Drain and add to tomato mixture. Simmer for 15 minutes. Season to taste.

Sear lamb rumps in a heavy-based fry-pan on high heat until brown on all sides. Place in a moderate oven (180°C) for about 15 minutes. Remove. Let rest for 5 minutes.

To serve: divide lentils evenly between four bowls. Slice lamb rumps and place on lentils. Top with Pumpkin Pickle and Tahini Yoghurt.

Serves 4

The Balcony Restaurant at Vasse Felix overlooks well-ordered rows of beautifully manicured vineyards. There is also a funky café, a striking modern art gallery and a wonderful underground cellar door.

Margaret River Marron Tails

GRILLED WITH LIME BUTTER,
SERVED ON SALAD OF ROCKET AND GRILLED MANGO
WITH YELLOW PEPPER DRESSING

Marrons
  18 marrons (fresh-water crayfish), each 100g
  200g butter
  4 limes
  salt and pepper

  Butterfly marron tails. Place on a grilling tray.
Blend butter, zest and juice of 1 lime, salt and
pepper in a processor to make a smooth paste.
Smear paste over marron flesh.

Yellow Pepper Dressing
  2 medium-sized yellow capsicums
  60ml white vinegar
  3 egg yolks
  60g Dijon mustard
  300ml olive oil

  Remove seeds and stems from capsicums.
Remove inner flesh, retaining outer skin for garnish.
Cook capsicum flesh with vinegar until tender.
Cool. Purée in a processor. Blend in egg yolks and
mustard. Motor on, slowly add oil until the
dressing thickens.
  Cut capsicum skins into fine julienne strips.
Place in iced water to curl.

Salad
  300g rocket
  100g sliced bread (or croutons)
  olive oil
  3 mangoes
  butter
  60g shaved parmesan
  bronze fennel leaves to garnish

  Wash rocket, drain and refrigerate to crisp.
  For croutons, cut bread into small cubes.
Drizzle with oil and bake in the oven until golden.
  Peel mangoes. Cut a slice from each side. Cut
each slice in half. Sauté mango slices in a little
butter in a hot pan to lightly brown.

  To assemble: grill marron tails for 10 minutes
until all flesh is cooked.
  Place 50g rocket on each serving plate. Drizzle
with dressing. Add marron (3 per plate), sliced
mango, croutons and shaved parmesan. Garnish
each with half a lime, some capsicum julienne
and bronze fennel.

Serves 6

*The bright colours of Western Australia's native flowers are
matched by the vivid expressions of local produce like this rich
dish of marron tails from Voyager Estate.*

RECIPE PREPARED BY
SAUL ATKINSON
VOYAGER ESTATE, MARGARET RIVER

WINE

Voyager Estate 1999 Sauvignon Blanc Semillon
*This blend of grapes excels here, giving a wine
that is a pleasing combination of ripe fruit
flavours and fine acidity. The Voyager Estate
style has pungent, herbaceous, lemony aromas
with softer tropical fruit flavours on the
palate, making it a perfect partner
for shellfish or crustaceans.*

Japanese Peppered Beef Sirloin

WITH BRAISED MUSHROOMS

50g Japanese or Szechwan peppercorns
4 beef sirloins steaks, trimmed of fat
oil and butter
1 shallot, peeled, chopped
200g assorted mushrooms, sliced
100ml dashi stock
25g miso paste
1 clove garlic, peeled, chopped

Asparagus Tempura
8 thin asparagus spears
light batter
oil for frying

To serve
4 tablespoons hollandaise sauce
a little wasabi paste to taste
enoki mushrooms to garnish

The steak: roast the peppercorns in a hot oven for 2–3 minutes until aromatic. Crush peppercorns. Press the pepper on to the steaks.
  Cook steaks in a hot pan with a little oil and butter, until they are to your liking. Remove from the pan and keep warm.

Braised Mushrooms: in the same pan cook chopped shallot for 2 minutes. Add mushrooms and cook until soft. Add dashi stock and simmer for 2 minutes. Stir in miso paste and garlic.

Asparagus: cut asparagus spears in halves. Dip in light batter and deep-fry until crisp.

To assemble: bring the braised mushrooms back to the boil. Spoon on to 4 warm plates.
  Slice steaks and place on the mushrooms.
  Serve with asparagus tempura and hollandaise sauce flavoured with a touch of wasabi paste. Garnish with enoki mushrooms.

Serves 4

RECIPE PREPARED BY
NEAL JACKSON
JACKSON'S, PERTH

WINE

Vasse Felix 1999 Margaret River Shiraz
Neal Jackson of Jackson's Restaurant believes that Margaret River Shiraz has been underrated for years and he cites this Vasse Felix vintage as proof of how good it can be – a full, rich, spicy wine with integrated vanillin oak and plum fruit, superbly complementing the rich flavours of beef sirloin.

Opiate, a classic expression of Margaret River Sauvignon Blanc, is produced exclusively for another of Perth's popular spots, Mark Rogers' buzzing high-ceilinged café, bistro and bar at 44 King Street.

Cotechino and Fennel Broth

100g black-eyed beans
1 large onion, peeled, finely diced
1 large fennel bulb, diced
4 inner stalks of celery, diced
3 cloves garlic, peeled, very finely chopped
200g butternut, peeled, seeds removed,
   diced
3 sprigs thyme
100ml extra virgin olive oil
2 litres chicken stock
salt and cracked pepper
1 cotechino sausage, about 500g*
100g swiss chard (silver beet)
100g parmesan, shaved

Soak dried beans in water overnight. Drain.
Sweat onion, fennel, celery, garlic, butternut and thyme leaves with olive oil for 10 minutes.
Add chicken stock. Bring to the boil and add black-eyed beans. Turn heat down and simmer for 20 minutes or until beans are soft. Season to taste.
Put the cotechino into 2 litres of boiling water for 15–20 minutes to remove excess fat.
Take the cotechino out of the water, dry with a cloth and add the whole sausage to the soup and let sit until ready to serve.

To serve: take cotechino out of the soup, remove skin then thinly slice the sausage.
Blanch swiss chard leaves in broth for 1 minute, then remove and drain.
Pour soup into bowls, making sure there are more vegetables than liquid. Place swiss chard on the vegetables. Add 3 slices of cotechino to each bowl. Place some shaved parmesan on top. Drizzle extra virgin olive oil around the soup.

Serves 8

*Cotechino (plural: cotechini), an Italian fresh pork sausage, quite large, usually seasoned with nutmeg, cloves, salt and pepper.

RECIPE PREPARED BY
CHRIS TAYLOR AND MARK HAYNES
FRASER'S RESTAURANT, PERTH

WINE

*Houghton 1996 Jack Mann
Cabernet Sauvignon Shiraz*

This special release wine made to commemorate Houghton's founding father is a rich and complex beauty, dark and heavy with scents of chocolate and fruit. The palate is bursting with ripe berry fruit backed by strong, supple tannins.

Fraser's Restaurant, set in King's Park, overlooks the stunning Perth skyline and the Swan River. Open blue skies, tall trees and air as clean as a whistle — it's hard to imagine a more perfect city setting.

Gnocchi and White Castello Sauce

SERVED ON A FRESH TOMATO SAUCE

8 medium-sized, floury potatoes (e.g. desirée)
2 tablespoons butter
1kg fresh ricotta
1⁄2 cup cream
100g grated parmesan cheese
pinch of salt
4–5 cups plain white flour

Boil potatoes in their skins until well cooked. Peel potatoes while they are still hot, then pass them through a potato ricer or food mill (mouli-legumes) with the butter. Pass potato through the mill again with ricotta. Mix well, pour in cream, then fold in parmesan cheese and salt.

Add small amounts of flour and mix with a fork. Keep adding flour, while mixing with your hands, until you get the right consistency (soft but dry enough to roll).

Roll out and cut into 2cm squares. Shape on a wooden gnocchi board.

Drop gnocchi into boiling, salted water, allow them to rise to the surface, then boil for 30 seconds. Remove with a slotted spoon and drain.

Fresh Tomato Sauce
   2.5kg tomatoes, peeled
   20g (about 1 cup) fresh basil
   1 onion, peeled, finely chopped
   2 cloves garlic, peeled, finely chopped
   olive oil
   2 teaspoons brown sugar
   salt and pepper

Process tomatoes and basil to a smooth consistency. Sauté onion and garlic in a little olive oil in a saucepan. Add tomato and basil, sugar, salt and pepper. Bring to the boil and cook rapidly, stirring frequently, for 45 minutes.

Ada Scaffidi presides over the kitchens of Altos, Perth's paean to authentic Italian cuisine and wine, while son Steve runs front-of-house. The upbeat, modern deco style of this ever-popular restaurant is both stylish and welcoming.

White Castello Sauce
   600ml cream
   80g white castello cheese
   50g finely grated parmesan
   20g (about 1 cup) basil
   15g rocket

Heat cream in a stainless steel pot to just below boiling point then whisk in white castello cheese. Remove from heat once the cheese is completely emulsified. Sprinkle in 40g parmesan, whisking to avoid lumps. Simmer to reduce by a quarter.

To serve: add cooked, drained gnocchi to White Castello Sauce, then add remaining 10g parmesan cheese. Add basil and rocket chiffonnade (finely sliced), toss, and serve on Fresh Tomato Sauce.

Serves 12

WINE

Umani Rochi Jorio 1998
Umani Rochi is an established Italian estate of some renown, whose 1998 Jorio is a characteristic Montepulciano d'Abruzzo — there are flavours of plums and wild cherries with great softness and balance.
It is also, according to Steve, 'a great accompaniment to Mum's Gnocchi'.

RECIPE PREPARED BY
ADA SCAFFIDI
ALTOS, SUBIACO

173

You're never far from the water in Tasmania, whether it is the sea or one of its many lakes and rivers.

Tasmania

Australia's island state can tend to be something of an afterthought in mainland awareness; indeed, it is not unheard of for Tasmania to be left off maps of Australia when Sydney-centric media depict the country in newspapers or on TV. The only regular exposure it seems to get is on weather forecasts, usually as the recipient of the coolest, wettest and windiest weather on the continent.

While this hardly seems fair, there are plenty of people secretly pleased that the majority seem to know little and care even less about Tassie. After all, if everyone realised just how beautiful it was, it wouldn't stay unspoilt for long.

Dramatic coastline; grassy plains; lakes, forests and mountains; white sandy beaches; orchards, vineyards, hop fields and lush pastures; quaint towns and vibrant cities – all can be found on this southern outcrop.

The climate is indeed cool, changeable and heavily influenced by the surrounding seas. While this does not give as easy a climate in which to grow grapes as warmer parts of Australia, it does provide the ideal conditions for elegance in certain varieties, most notably Chardonnay, Pinot Noir and, to a lesser degree, Riesling.

The cool conditions and long ripening period allow complex flavours and tight structure to develop in the fruit. These are just the characters needed for great sparkling wine, so perhaps it's no surprise that Tasmania is fast becoming the capital of Australia's premium fizz production.

The other star performer is varietal Pinot Noir (in other words, used as a solo red instead of in a sparkling blend). This notoriously tricky grape thrives here, and increasingly good examples are coming out of Tasmania's 70 or so wineries. Other fine wines are being made with Pinot Gris, Gewurztraminer, Merlot and, in the right spots, Cabernet Sauvignon.

This blessed isle yields fine foods to go with its elegant wines as well. Seafood, salmon, game, cheeses, honey, fruit and produce are all excellent. Tasmania is far from an afterthought – make sure you discover what the rest of Australia is missing.

The general store in the quaint country town of Piper's Brook, above. Set amid rolling green hills, the area was once a prime cattle and sheep grazing area. Today it is one of the main hubs of the booming Tasmanian wine industry, though the resident geese at Pipers Brook Vineyard seem unaware of this.

Roasted Red Pepper Salad

(PART OF THE ANTIPASTI)

2 large red capsicums (peppers)
1 clove garlic, peeled, finely chopped
juice of 1/2 lemon
olive oil
freshly ground black pepper
salt flakes
anchovy fillets (optional)

Cut the capsicums in half lengthwise. Remove seeds, pith and any stem. Flatten each half and place, skin sides up, on a sheet of foil under a very hot grill until the skins are well blackened.

Remove foil and capsicums from under the grill. Loosely wrap the capsicums in the foil and leave them to sweat for 10 minutes. Peel away and discard skins.

Cut the flesh into strips. Dress with the garlic, lemon juice, olive oil, pepper and salt flakes. Mix well and leave to marinate for at least one hour.

Optional: cut several anchovy fillets in half lengthwise and gently fold through the salad.

Arrange on a platter with a handful of baby spinach leaves, black olives, marinated artichokes, prosciutto, salami, roasted eggplant, roasted beet-root relish and crusty bread.

WINE

Pipers Brook Vineyard 2000 Riesling
Andrew Pirie and Pipers Brook Vineyard have been the driving force behind Tasmania's rapid growth as a serious premium wine region. This Riesling is aromatic with exotic fruit characters and complex, rich fruit flavours, and goes well with The Winery Café's popular Roasted Red Pepper Salad.

RECIPE PREPARED BY
DANIEL ALPS
THE WINERY CAFÉ, PIPERS BROOK VINEYARD

Seared Chicken Breast

WITH ROAST PUMPKIN, SEMI-DRIED TOMATOES,
HUMMUS AND PESTO

Semi-dried Tomatoes
    6 roma tomatoes
    1 teaspoon each finely chopped thyme,
        rosemary, chives, sage
    1 tablespoon each sea salt and sugar

Halve tomatoes and place on a wire rack.
Sprinkle with herb, sugar and salt mixture and
place in the oven with pilot light on (or on
lowest setting) overnight.

Pesto
    200g basil leaves
    1/2 teaspoon sea salt
    150ml extra virgin olive oil
    125g roasted pine nuts
    5 cloves garlic, peeled
    black pepper
    150g grated parmesan

Process basil, salt and 50ml of olive oil until
a paste is formed. Add pine nuts, garlic and
pepper and pulse to a paste. With motor running,
drizzle in remaining oil until smooth. Remove
and stir in the parmesan. Check seasoning.

Chicken Breasts
    6 boneless chicken breasts, skin on
    3 tablespoons mixed mustard
    300ml olive oil
    3 tablespoons chopped rosemary
    salt and pepper

Mix together mustard, olive oil, rosemary and
seasoning. Coat chicken breasts with this mixture.
Pan-fry both sides until nicely golden. Finish in a
moderate oven for 5 minutes. Rest in a warm
place for a further 5 minutes.

To serve
    chunks of roast pumpkin
    hummus

To assemble: on each plate place a bed of roast
pumpkin. Top with a chicken breast. Add semi-
dried tomatoes. Top the chicken with some
hummus and pesto.

Serves 6

RECIPE PREPARED BY
DANIEL ALPS
NINTH ISLAND WINERY RESTAURANT

*Pennyroyal Village tourist apartments, set back into the cliffs
above Launceston, illustrate the typical Dutch-style architecture
of this area. Classic houses in similar style run the length of
the Tamar River here.*

WINE

Ninth Island 1998 Chardonnay
*The ripe, tropical fruit flavours, with hints
of peach and passionfruit, and the fine acidity
of the Ninth Island Chardonnay provide
a good match for the winery restaurant's
own mustard-coated chicken with pumpkin,
pesto and hummus.*

Cumquat
Ice Cream

WITH CHOUX PASTRY AND MACERATED ORANGES

Ice Cream

 1 vanilla pod
 20 egg yolks
 400g sugar
 2 litres cream
 250g brandied cumquats

Split vanilla pod and scrape out seeds. Add seeds to egg yolks and sugar and beat (best done with an electric mixer) until double in volume.

Heat cream with vanilla pod to just under boiling point. Add cream to egg mixture and stir until well combined. Place back on low heat and stir continuously with a wooden spoon until the custard is thick enough to coat the spoon. This should take 10–15 minutes. Transfer immediately to a bowl and allow to cool.

Add brandied cumquats to the ice cream base before churning and freezing.

Choux Pastry

 250ml water
 60g butter
 pinch of salt
 250g flour
 zest of 1 orange
 4 eggs

Bring water, butter and salt slowly to the boil. Remove from heat. Sift in flour and work the mixture over moderate heat until a thin crust forms on the bottom of the saucepan. Transfer mixture to a clean saucepan and let rest for 2 minutes.

Add zest and then eggs, one at a time, beating each one in thoroughly with a wooden spoon before adding the next.

Pipe the mixture into 12 small mounds on a baking tray. Sprinkle lightly with water.

Bake in the oven at 220°C for 20 minutes.

Cool on a cake rack.

Toffee Filigree: stir and heat 500g caster sugar with 250ml water until golden (or 130°C, hard crack stage). Plunge pot into cold water to halt cooking. Let rest for 2 minutes. Drizzle desired shapes on to non-stick baking paper and let set.

RECIPE PREPARED BY
DANIEL ALPS
THE STRATHLYNN, STRATHLYNN WINE CENTRE

This Flinders Island Milk-fed Lamb with Beetroot Risotto from the Strathlynn menu is another speciality of local chef Daniel Alps, who divides his many talents between several wineries and restaurants.

The restaurant and the views at Strathlynn are breathtaking, overlooking the glinting Tamar River.

WINE

Ninth Island 1999 White Frontignac
This fresh, grapey, floral light white is delicate and delightful with the delicious cumquat ice cream. One of the few wines actually to taste of grapes!

Serving options: slice each choux bun into three. Place one slice on a serving plate and top with a ball of cumquat ice cream. Repeat layers, finishing with the top of the choux bun. Sprinkle with couverture chocolate shavings and serve with macerated orange segments. Or omit chocolate and serve with vanilla crème anglaise, biscotti, and toffee filigree shapes to garnish.

Serves 12

Chinese
Five Spice Soufflé

WITH POACHED NASHI AND HONEY TUILES

2 nashi pears

125g raw sugar

1 cinnamon quill

150g butter

150g plain flour

500ml milk

1/2 teaspoon Chinese five spice powder

200g caster sugar

soft butter and caster sugar for preparing moulds

6 eggs, separated

Peel, halve and core nashi pears. Poach gently in a pot of hot water with raw sugar and cinnamon quill until nashi are soft. Leave to cool in the liquid, then drain nashi and cut into dice. Set half aside for garnish.

Melt butter in a heavy-based saucepan. Add flour and cook, stirring constantly with a wooden spoon, for 5 minutes. Gradually add the milk, stirring constantly, and bring to the boil. Cook, stirring, until thick and smooth. Add five spice powder mixed with caster sugar. When sugar is dissolved, set the mixture aside to cool slightly.

Meanwhile grease 8 small soufflé moulds with soft butter, making sure you grease right to the rims. Sprinkle in caster sugar until coated, then shake out excess.

Beat egg yolks into the five spice sauce, blending them in thoroughly.

Whip egg whites until soft peaks form. Mix a large spoonful of egg whites into the sauce base with half of the diced nashi pears. Gently but firmly fold in remaining whites. Carefully spoon the mixture into the moulds, making sure none touches the rims, until moulds are 3/4 full.

Stand moulds in a water bath. Bake in a moderately hot oven (190–200°C) until soufflés are golden and risen. Remove soufflés and allow to sink and cool. Remove carefully from the moulds. (At this stage they can be stored in the fridge until needed.)

To reheat, place soufflés upside down on a greased baking tray. Bake at 190–200°C for about 25 minutes, or until puffed and risen again.

Serve immediately with remaining diced nashi pears, whipped cream and Honey Tuiles (recipe follows).

Serves 8

WINE

1999 Wellington Iced Riesling

Gifted winemaker Andrew Hood makes this luscious and concentrated dessert wine by freeze-concentrating the juice from his Riesling grapes before fermentation.
The result is an intense and complex gem, well matched with the soufflé's subtle spices.

Honey Tuiles

110g caster sugar

1 teaspoon vanilla essence

75g sifted flour

2 eggs

30g very soft butter

10g (1 1/2 teaspoons) honey

Place all ingredients into the bowl of a mixer and beat until just smooth.

Spread thinly into templates or circles drawn on silicon paper (or non-stick baking sheets) on oven trays. Bake in a slow oven (140–160°C) until golden brown.

Carefully remove with a palette knife and bend into the required shape while still hot. If tuiles harden before you have shaped them, return them briefly to the oven to soften again.

Makes 40 small tuiles or 20 larger ones

RECIPE PREPARED BY
FIONA HOSKIN
FEE AND ME, LAUNCESTON

Lime and Sugar Cured Salmon

WITH GREEN MANGO SALSA, DRESSED NOODLES
AND LIME AND PEPPER PASTE

240g Tasmanian salmon, very thinly sliced
   into neat, 2.5cm squares
2 teaspoons Tasmanian salmon caviar

Salmon Marinade
   juice of 1 lime
   50g brown sugar
   50ml light oil
   50ml white wine vinegar
   1 1/2 teaspoons chopped coriander root and stalks
   freshly ground black pepper

Salmon: mix together all marinade ingredients. Add salmon and marinate for 10 minutes only.

Green Mango Salsa
   1/2 green mango, peeled, finely diced
   1/2 red onion, finely diced
   2 teaspoons brown sugar
   1 teaspoon light oil
   2 teaspoons finely chopped Vietnamese mint

Salsa: combine all ingredients.

Lime and Pepper Paste
   Mix salt, cracked white pepper and lime juice
   to a paste.

Noodles
   2 cups cucumber 'noodles'*

Dressing
   2 teaspoons each rice wine vinegar and
      light oil
   1 teaspoon each caster sugar and lime juice

To assemble: toss noodles with dressing ingredients. Spin noodles in the centre of each plate. Layer marinated salmon squares around the edge and top with mango salsa. Dab a teaspoon of lime and pepper paste on the plate between the salmon stacks. Top each noodle mound with a teaspoon of salmon caviar.

Serves 2

*Fine vermicelli-like shreds cut from cucumber using a mandoline slicer. Alternatively, use fine cellophane noodles, blanched. Or use a mixture of the two.

RECIPE PREPARED BY
DON CAMERON
STILLWATER RIVER CAFÉ

The Batman suspension bridge over the Tamar, above, one of the many fish-rich rivers that streak Tasmania's landscape. The Stillwater River Café sits right on the banks of the Tamar, with yachts and water birds all around.

Tasmania's rural heartland

The road from Launceston to Hobart runs through the heart of Tasmania. This is lush sheep and cattle country, dotted with small villages, townships and quaint wooden farmhouses. Plum in the centre is the Red Bridge in Campbelltown, designed by a convict in 1838 and built by his cellmates. Driving is a pleasure, with long, empty roads taking you past beautiful vistas like the vineyards at Winstead, where award-winning Pinot Noir and Riesling are made.

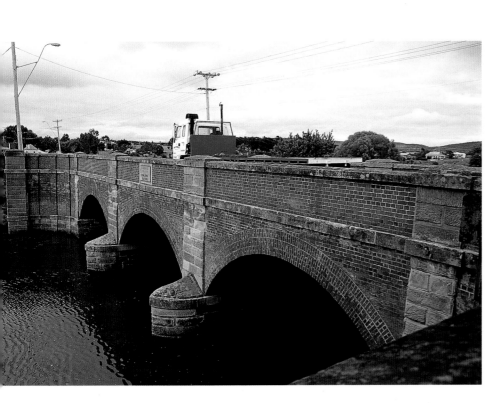

Supreme of Salmon
à la Marinière

WITH FRESH BLUE MUSSELS AND
MAGHREBIA COUSCOUS

72 fresh blue (black) mussels
50g each finely diced carrot, shallot, leek, celery
200ml white wine
500ml fish stock
butter
1 leek, washed, sliced
2 cloves garlic, crushed
salt and freshly ground pepper
500g maghrebia (large, pearl couscous)*
6 portions salmon (skinless, boneless), each 150g
2 tomatoes, skinned, de-seeded
1/2 bunch roughly chopped herbs

Wash and beard mussels. Place in a pot with diced carrot, shallot, leek, celery and the wine. Cover and cook until shells open. Remove the mussels and discard top shells. Retain the cooking liquid.

Combine the mussel-cooking liquid with an equal amount of fish stock, add a knob of butter and simmer to slightly intensify flavour.

Sauté leek and garlic in a little butter to soften. Season to taste. Cook maghrebia couscous in boiling, salted water for 10 minutes until just tender. Refresh, then strain off water. Add couscous to sautéed leek and garlic.

Poach the salmon in the fish stock mixture for about 5 minutes. Add mussels in the half shell with finely diced carrot, shallot, leek and celery, just to heat through.

To serve: place couscous in the middle of each large, deep plate. Arrange 10–12 mussels in the half shell around the outside. Place salmon in the centre. Pour cooking juices with vegetables evenly over. Garnish with diced flesh of the tomatoes and chopped fresh herbs.

Serves 6

*Maghrebia is large couscous (made from durum wheat semolina grains, formed into sago-size balls) available from Middle Eastern food stores.

RECIPE PREPARED BY
MARK WILSDON
A SPLASH OF PARIS, HOBART

The Salamanca Markets are a highlight of any visit to Hobart for locals and visitors alike. Every Saturday morning, as the sun rises on Salamanca Place, hundreds of street stalls are set up to sell everything from homemade honey to antique woodworking tools. Most striking of all are the colourful stalls of the Vietnamese garden farmers, piled high with their fruit, vegetables and produce.

WINE

A Splash of Paris, Moorilla Estate Reserve Pinot Noir

Mark and Elizabeth Wilsdon put their own label on Moorilla Estate's Reserve Pinot Noir for their Splash of Paris boardwalk brasserie. It's a spicy wine with gamy overtones, and it goes well with this hearty salmon and mussel dish.

Roasted Tasmanian Duck

WITH MUSHROOM AND CORIANDER ROSTI AND RED ONION CONFIT

4 whole duck breasts with wing bones,
    each 180–200g
salt and pepper
beef jus

Rosti
    100g cooked, mashed kennebec potatoes
        (or other floury potatoes)
    100g raw, grated kennebec potato
    40g oyster mushrooms
    40g honey brown mushrooms
    40g straw mushrooms
    2 tablespoons chopped coriander leaves
    4 eggs
    flour
    salt and pepper

Red Onion Confit
    4 red onions, peeled, finely sliced
    50g butter
    100g brown sugar
    300ml red wine

The Moorilla winery, which sits on its own peninsula jutting out into the Derwent River, was founded in 1956 by Claudio Alcorso, one of the modern-day Tasmanian wine pioneers. These fermentation and storage tanks are a reminder that, although good winemaking will always be an art, it takes hard-nosed science to achieve the results.

Rosti: combine the mashed and grated potatoes. Add chopped mushrooms and coriander. Mix in eggs, then enough flour to give the desired consistency (firm enough to shape into cakes). Add seasoning. Shape into 4 flat cakes, about 10cm in diameter.
Place rosti on a greased baking tray. Bake at about 200°C for about 12 minutes, until golden.

Red Onion Confit: sweat onions with butter and brown sugar until soft. Slowly add wine and cook until dark red in colour.

To roast duck: season the duck breasts and place service-side up (to ensure that the fat keeps the breast moist during cooking) in a roasting pan. Roast at 200°C for 15 minutes. Allow to rest in a warm area for 10 minutes.

To serve: Place a rosti on each plate. Place a duck breast on top of each rosti with the onion confit. Finish with hot beef jus.

Serves 4

RECIPE PREPARED BY
NICHOLAS DUNN
MOORILLA ESTATE, HOBART

Tasmanian Ocean Trout

ON VEGETABLE PAYSANNE WITH SEARED SCALLOPS AND
SAFFRON BRODO

400ml fish stock made with genuine saffron
    strands
salt and pepper
2 portions Tasmanian ocean trout, skin on,
    each 200g
oil and butter
10 plump Tasmanian scallops, cleaned
200g prepared leek, capsicum and zucchini
    cut into kite-shapes, 2cm in diameter,
    carrot cut as 'flowers'
2 sprigs fresh Italian parsley

Strain the saffron fish stock and season to taste.
Place in a clean pot ready to cook vegetables.

Seal the ocean trout (skin side up), in a little
oil and butter, then turn and season. Bake at
200°C for 4 minutes.

Heat another pan until hot. Add 1 teaspoon
of oil and a tiny knob of butter and sear the
scallops for 20 seconds.

While fish is cooking, return the stock (the
brodo) to a simmer, add vegetables and cook
for 2 minutes.

To assemble: warm two large, wide bowls. In
the middle of each bowl place vegetables in a
neat mound. Place ocean trout, skin side uppermost, on top of vegetables. Arrange seared
scallops around the sides and gently pour saffron
brodo over the seafood until bowls are half full.
Garnish each with a sprig of parsley.

Serves 2

RECIPE PREPARED BY
MARK GOOKLUCK
LAMB PREPARED BY GRAHAM L. SMITH

ALEXANDER'S RESTAURANT
LENNA OF HOBART

*Another speciality at Alexander's is Rack of Spring Lamb with
Semi-dried Tomato Crust served on a Roast Vegetable Stack
with Skordalia and Capocollo and Caper Jus, shown above.*

WINES

Freycinet Vineyard 1998 Chardonnay
From a small, family-owned vineyard on
the Freycinet Peninsula in the warmer
East Coast sub-region, this is a ripe, buttery,
peachy Chardonnay with well-balanced oak
and good length. It is a good foil for the
delicate ocean trout and scallop dish.

Kinvarra Estate 1998 Pinot Noir
One of many wines made by Andrew Hood
for Tasmania's legion of small growers,
this one is from David and Sue Bevan's
Kinvarra Estate Vineyards.
It has classic Pinot characters, with
fine tannins, spicy fruit and subtle use of oak,
ideal for a rack of spring lamb.

Queensland

Queensland winemakers could be forgiven for having a very large, very heavy communal chip on their shoulders. After all, how often have you heard anyone say 'Wow, Queensland – that's where they make all the great wine, isn't it?'.

For most people, it's a case of think Queensland, think Gold Coast or the tropics, and certainly not winemaking, but the truth is very different. Vines have been planted here since the 1850s and, though much of the early production was small scale, the industry has grown steadily since the 1960s.

The Granite Belt is Queensland's longest-established and most premium wine region. It is also one of the most picturesque in the country, at a high altitude with steep granite outcrops and five national parks nearby, plus plenty of small, welcoming family-run cellar doors.

Spectacular views also abound around Mount Tamborine, just a short drive into the hills behind the flashy attractions of the Gold Coast beach scene, while if you want to see large-scale vineyard development at its quickest, head for South Burnett a couple of hours north-west of Brisbane.

There is a thriving food and cooking scene here, too, using some excellent regional ingredients – tropical fruit, macadamia nuts and fantastic seafood abound. So next time you think of Queensland, remember the wines and take some time to find them.

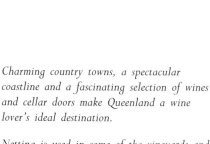

Charming country towns, a spectacular coastline and a fascinating selection of wines and cellar doors make Queenland a wine lover's ideal destination.

Netting is used in some of the vineyards and serves a dual purpose, keeping voracious tropical birds at bay and shading the grapes when the sun is at its fiercest.

Seared Queensland Scallops

ON RISOTTO NERI WITH SLOW-ROASTED TOMATOES

Risotto Neri

    500ml fish stock

    100ml squid ink

    3 large brown onions, peeled, finely diced

    100ml extra virgin olive oil

    130g salted butter

    400g arborio or vialone nano rice

    200ml Chardonnay

    5 roma tomatoes

    a little chopped thyme and garlic

    25 Queensland scallops, opened, cleaned,
      roe off

    1 teaspoon curry powder

    100ml extra virgin olive oil

    tomato concassé

    zest of 2 lemons

    chives

    olive oil to garnish

Risotto Neri: bring fish stock and squid ink to a simmer.

In a heavy-based pot sauté onions in the olive oil with 80g of the butter until soft and translucent. Add rice and lightly fry until pale golden.

Add Chardonnay and stir until absorbed. Then slowly add hot stock, about 80–100ml at a time, ensuring that it is absorbed between additions. Continue to cook, adding stock, until rice is al dente. Stir in remaining butter and remove from heat.

To slow-roast tomatoes: halve roma tomatoes. place cut sides up in a baking dish. Sprinkle with chopped thyme and garlic. Roast at 50°C for 5 hours.

Scallops: preheat a heavy, oiled pan until smoking. Roll scallops in curry powder and olive oil to lightly coat then sear in the pan, being careful as it can flame up. Do not over-cook the scallops; they should be opaque in the middle.

To serve: arrange risotto in the centre of the plates. Top each with 5 scallops. Garnish with slow-roasted tomatoes, tomato concassé, lemon zest, chives and a drizzle of your best olive oil.

Serves 5

RECIPE PREPARED BY
CAMERON MATTHEWS
RESTAURANT LURLEEN'S, MOUNT COTTON
ESTATE

WINE

*Mount Cotton Estate 2000
Stradbrooke Chardonnay*

*With noted winemakers Adam Chapman and Alain Rousseau at the helm, it's no surprise that this Mount Cotton Chardonnay is a classic example.
Ripe tropical fruit characters with notes of fine French oak on the nose give way to a full-bodied, rich mouthful with buttery, yeasty flavours. Perfect with scallops.*

Fine views and spectacular scenery abound at Mount Cotton Estate, one of the most innovative and exciting new wineries in Queensland.

Crème Brûlée

WITH FRESH FRUIT

1 teaspoon vanilla extract
600ml cream
6 egg yolks
1/4 cup caster sugar
extra caster sugar

fresh raspberries, strawberries, dates,
    lychees and grapes

Warm vanilla and cream in a heat-proof bowl
over simmering water.

Beat egg yolks and 1/4 cup of sugar with an
electric mixer until light and creamy. Slowly
add warm cream to egg mixture, continuing to
lightly beat.

Place the mixture in a saucepan over medium
heat and stir constantly without boiling for 5
minutes, or until it starts to thicken.

Divide the custard between 6 small heat-proof
dishes. Cover and refrigerate for 4 hours or
overnight.

Sprinkle custards with extra caster sugar and
place under a hot grill for 2 minutes or until
golden brown. Return to the refrigerator for
2–3 hours before serving.

To serve: place each Crème Brûlée on a platter
and arrange the fruit around as you wish.

Serves 6

RECIPE PREPARED BY
ROBYN HENDERSON AND MARY PUGLISI
BALLANDEAN ESTATE WINES, QUEENSLAND

WINE

Ballandean Estate 1999 Late Harvest Sylvaner
A superb sticky made with an Alsace grape
that seems to have found its second home
in Queensland. Mark Ravenscroft is following
in Angelo Puglisi's ground-breaking footsteps
with this intense, luscious mouthful of ripe
apricot and tropical fruit flavours and
a crisp, clean finish. Delicious!

Ballandean Estate has been at the forefront of the
development of winemaking in Queensland's Granite Belt
from the start. Its wildly popular tasting room and
restaurant make it well worth a visit.

WINE

Platypus 2000 Cabernet Merlot

This soft, easy-drinking red is made from a blend of Cabernet Sauvignon, Merlot, Chambourcin and Shiraz. Its upfront berry characters and red fruit flavours make it a good match with Darrell Lovely's char-grilled roo and plum chilli dish.

Char-grilled Kangaroo Fillet

WITH ILLAWARRA PLUM CHILLI SAUCE

360g kangaroo fillet
200ml honey
200ml beer

Plum Chilli Sauce
400g plums
200g sugar
400ml water
6 tablespoons macadamia nut oil
1 onion, diced
2 teaspoons crushed garlic
2 red chillies, sliced
2 teaspoons brown sugar

extra macadamia nut oil
salt and cracked pepper
2 bunches warrigal greens (bush spinach)
juice of 1 lime
2 pinches wattle seed powder for decoration

Slice kangaroo fillet into thin strips and place in a small bowl or container. Add honey and beer. Cover and refrigerate for at least 2 hours, or preferably overnight.

Plum Chilli Sauce: place plums, sugar and water in a saucepan and bring to the boil. Simmer for 20 minutes. Remove stones then purée plums in a blender.
Heat macadamia nut oil in a pan and sauté diced onion, garlic and chilli until onion is transparent. Add brown sugar and plum purée and simmer to reduce and thicken.

Brush a very hot char-grill or hot-plate with macadamia nut oil. Add kangaroo strips and cook for 1 minute on each side. Season with salt and pepper. Do not over-cook kangaroo as it will toughen.

Wash the greens in cold water, shaking off excess. Toss greens in a bowl with a sprinkle of cracked pepper, macadamia nut oil and lime juice.

To serve: centre the greens on the plates. Place kangaroo over the greens. The chef adds a wedge of Pumpkin Cheesecake to each plate. Drizzle plum chilli sauce around the kangaroo. Optional: garnish with sliced red or yellow capsicum. Dust the plate rims with wattle seed powder for decoration.

Serves 2

Pumpkin Cheesecake

1 butternut or small pumpkin
4 eggs
100ml cream
100ml ricotta
salt, pepper

Base
150g chilled butter
300g plain flour
50–80ml water

Filling: peel butternut and discard seeds. Steam or boil butternut until soft. Drain and mash well. Beat in the eggs then add cream and ricotta. Season with salt and pepper to taste.

Base: Rub butter into flour to make the consistency of breadcrumbs. Slowly add water, mixing to a dough. Compact into a ball, cover and refrigerate for 30 minutes.
Roll out pastry and line two 14cm diameter flan tins. Bake blind at 160°C for 10 minutes, or until golden. Fill with butternut mixture. Bake at 160°C for 40 minutes, or until set. Cut into wedges. Serve hot or cold.

Serves 8

RECIPES PREPARED BY
DARRELL LOVELY
CANUNGRA VALLEY VINEYARD RESTAURANT

The Canungra Valley Vineyard and Restaurant with a dramatic natural backdrop.

Wineries

The following are the wineries referred to in this book, listed alphabetically.

All Saints Estate
Tel: (02) 6033 1922; Fax: (02) 6033 3515;
Email: wine@allsaintswine.com.au

Ballandean Estate Winery
Tel: (07) 4684 1226; Fax: (07) 4684 1288;
Email: enquiries@ballandean-estate.com.au

Barak Estate
Tel: (03) 5978 8439; Fax: (03) 5978 8439;
Email: barakestate@smartchat.net.au

Bethany Wines
Tel: (08) 8563 2086; Fax: (08) 8568 0046;
Email: bethany@bethany.com.au

Blue Pyrenees
Tel: (03) 5465 3202; Fax: (03) 5465 3529;
Email: mike.cutrupi@remy-cointreau.com

Brokenwood
Tel: (02) 4998 7559; Fax: (02) 4998 7893;
Email: graveyard@brokenwood.com.au

Brookland Valley Vineyard
Tel: (08) 9731 0400; Fax: (08) 9226 4110;
Email: vineyard@bvml.com.au

Brown Brothers Milawa Vineyard
Tel: (03) 5720 5500; Fax: (03) 5720 5511;
Email: bbmv@brown-brothers.com.au

Canungra Valley Vineyards
Tel: (07) 5543 4011; Fax: (07) 5543 4162;
Email: vineyard@oreillys.com.au

Capercaillie
Tel: (02) 4990 2904; Fax: (02) 4991 1886;
Email: capercaillie@hunterlink.net.au

Chain of Ponds
Tel: (08) 8389 1415; Fax: (08) 8389 1877;
Email: admin@chainofponds.com.au

Chambers Rosewood Winery
Tel: (02) 6032 8641; Fax: (02) 6032 8101;
Email: wchambers@netc.net.au

Chateau Tanunda
Tel: (08) 8563 3888; Fax: (08) 8563 1422

Cofield
Tel: (02) 6033 3798; Fax: (02) 6033 0798

Cope-Williams
Tel: (03) 5429 5428; Fax: (03) 5429 5655;
Email: winesales@cope-williams.com.au

Coriole
Tel: (08) 8323 8305; Fax: (08) 8323 9136;
Email: coriole@senet.com.au

Cowra Estate
Tel: (02) 6342 1136; Fax: (02) 6342 4286;
Email: cowraestate@ozemail.com.au

Craneford Wine Co
Tel: (08) 8564 0003; Fax: (08) 8564 0008;
Email: johnzilm@dove.net.au

Cullen Wines
Tel: (08) 9755 5277; Fax: (08) 9755 5550

De Bortoli
Tel: (03) 5965 2423; Fax: (03) 5965 2464;
Email: dbw@debortoli.com.au

Delatite
Tel: (03) 5775 2922; Fax: (03) 5775 2911

Diamond Valley Vineyards
Tel: (03) 9710 1484; Fax: (03) 9710 1369;
Email: enq@diamondvalley.com.au

Domaine Chandon
Tel: (03) 9739 1110; Fax: (03) 9739 1095;
Email: info@domainechandon.com.au

Eldredge Wines
Tel: (08) 8842 3086; Fax: (08) 8842 3086;
Email: bluechip@capri.net.au

Freycinet Vineyards
Tel: (03) 6257 8574; Fax: (03) 6257 8454;
Email: freycinetwines@tassie.net.au

Henschke
Tel: (08) 8564 8223; Fax:
(08) 8564 8294;
Email: henschke@dove.net.au

Highland Heritage Estate
Tel: (02) 6361 7381; Fax: (02) 6362 6183;
Email: daquino@netwit.net.au

Houghton Wine Company
Tel: (08) 9274 5100; Fax: (08) 9250 3872;
Email: corporate@brlhardy.com.au

Katnook Estate
Tel: (08) 8737 2394; Fax: (08) 8737 2397;
Email: katnook@wingara.com.au

Kellybrook Winery
Tel: (03) 9722 1304; Fax: (03) 9722 2092;
Email: kellybrook@ozemail.com.au

Kinvarra Estate
Tel: (03) 6286 1333; Fax: (03) 6286 2026;
Email: kinvarra@tasmail.com

Leasingham
Tel: (08) 8842 2555; Fax: (08) 8842 3293

Leeuwin Estate
Tel: (08) 9757 6253; Fax: (08) 9757 6364;
Email: info@leeuwinestate.com.au

Lillydale Vineyards
Tel: (03) 5964 2016; Fax: (03) 5964 3009;
Email: mcwines@mcwilliams.com.au

Lindemans
Tel: (08) 8737 2613; Fax: (08) 8737 2959

Majella
Tel: (08) 8736 3055; Fax: (08) 8736 3057;
Email: prof@penola.mtx.net.au

Malcolm Creek Vineyard
Tel: (08) 8389 3235; Fax: (08) 8389 3235

Marienburg Wines
Tel: (08) 8323 9666; Fax: (08) 8323 9600;
Email: cellardoor@marienburg.com.au

Mitchelton Wines
Tel: (03) 5736 2222; Fax: (03) 5736 2266;
Email: mitchelton@mitchelton.com.au

Moorilla Estate
Tel: (03) 6277 9900; Fax: (03) 6249 4093;
Email: moorilla.wine@tassie.net.au

Moorooduc Estate
Tel: (03) 5971 8506; Fax: (03) 5971 8550;
Email: moorooduc@ozemail.com.au

Morning Star Estate Winery
Tel: (03) 9787 7760; Fax: (03) 9787 7160
Email: morningstarestate@bigpond.com.au

Mountadam Vineyard
Tel: (08) 8564 1101; Fax:(08) 8564 1064;
Email: office@mountadam.com

Mount Cotton Estate
Tel: (07) 3206 2999; Fax: (07) 3206 0900;
Email: wines@mountcottonestate.com

Mount Pleasant Wines
Tel: (02) 4998 7505; Fax: (02) 4998 7761;
Email: mcwines@mcwilliams.com.au

Nepenthe Vineyards
Tel: (08) 8389 8039;
Email: pleske@nepenthe.com.au

Ninth Island Winery
Tel: (03) 6382 7122; Fax: (03) 6382 7225

Penfolds Wines
Tel: (08) 8568 9389; Fax: (08) 8568 9489

Penley Estate
Tel: (08) 8363 5500; Fax: (08) 8363 5366;
Email: penley@penley.com.au

Pepper Tree Wines
Tel: (02) 4998 7539; Fax: (02) 4998 7746;
Email: ptwinery@peppertreewines.com.au

Petaluma
Tel: (08) 8339 4122; Fax: (08) 8339 5253;
Email: petaluma@petaluma.com

Pheasant Farm Wines
Tel: (08) 8562 4477; Fax: (08) 8562 4757;
Email: farmshop@maggiebeer.com.au

Pikes Wines
Tel: (08) 8843 4370; Fax: (08) 8843 4353;
Email: info@pikeswines.com.au

Pipers Brook Vineyard
Tel: (03) 6332 4444; Fax: (03) 6382 7226;
Email: info@pbv.com.au

Poet's Corner
Tel: (02) 6373 3853; Fax: (02) 6373 3795

Red Hill Estate
Tel: (03) 5989 2838; Fax: (03) 5989 2855;
Email: info@redhillestate.com.au

Reilly's Wines
Tel: (08) 8843 9013; Fax: (08) 8843 9013;
Email: reillys@ozemail.com.au

Riverina Estate
Tel: (02) 6962 4122; Fax: (02) 6962 4628;
Email: info@riverinawines.com.au

Rosemount
Tel: (02) 6549 6400; Fax: (02) 6549 6499;
Email: mail@rosemountestates.com.au

Rymill Coonawarra
Tel: (08) 8736 5001; Fax: (08) 8736 5040;
Email: winery@rymill.com.au

Saltram Wine Estates
Tel: (08) 8564 3355; Fax: (08) 8564 3384

Seppelts Winery
Tel: (08) 8568 6200; Fax: (08) 8568 0204

Sevenhill Cellars
Tel: (08) 8843 4222; Fax: (08) 8843 4382;
Email: 7hillcel@rbe.net.au

Shaw and Smith
Tel: (08) 8398 0500; Fax: (08) 8398 0600;
Email: shawandsmith@shawandsmith.com

Skillogalee Wines
Tel: (08) 8843 4311; Fax: (08) 8843 4343;
Email: skilly@capri.net.au

St Hallett Wines
Tel: (08) 8563 7000; Fax: (08) 8563 7001;
Email: sthallett@sthallett.com.au

T'Gallant
Tel: (03) 5989 6565; Fax: (03) 5989 6577

The Hanging Rock Winery
Tel: (03) 5427 0542; Fax: (03) 5427 0310;
Email: HRW@hangingrock.com.au

Tyrrell's
Tel: (02) 4993 7000; Fax: (02) 4998 7723;
Email: admin@tyrrells.com.au

Vasse Felix
Tel: (08) 9756 5000; Fax: (08) 9755 5425;
Email: info@vassefelix.com.au

Villa Primavera
Tel: (03) 5989 2129; Fax: (03) 5989 2129

Voyager Estate
Tel: (08) 9757 6358; Fax: (08) 9757 6405;
Email: wine@voyagerestate.com.au

Wandin Valley Estate
Tel: (02) 4930 7317; Fax: (02) 4930 7814;
Email: wanval@ozemail.com.au

Wellington
Tel: (03) 6248 5844; Fax: (03) 6248 5855

Willow Creek Vineyard
Tel: (03) 5989 7448; Fax: (03) 5989 7584;
Email: admin@willow-creek.com.au

Wirra Wirra Vineyards
Tel: (08) 8323 8414; Fax: (08) 8323 8596;
Email: info@wirra.com.au

Woodstock Winery & Coterie
Tel: (08) 8383 0516; Fax: (08) 8383 0437;
Email: woodstock@woodstockwine.com.au

Yalumba
Tel: (08) 8561 3200; Fax: (08) 8561 3393;
Email: info@yalumba.com

Zema Estate
Tel: (08) 8736 3219; Fax: (08) 8736 3280; Email:
zemaestate@zema.com.au

Compiled by Peter Fuller & Associates

Restaurants

The following are the restaurants whose recipes are featured in this book, listed alphabetically, by state.

South Australia

Chain of Ponds
Tel: (08) 8389 1415; Fax: (08) 8389 1877

Chardonnay Lodge
Tel: (08) 8736 3309; Fax: (08) 8736 3383

Chloe's Restaurant
Tel: (08) 8362 2574; Fax: (08) 8363 1001

'Limeburner's Restaurant' at Marienburg Wines
Tel: (08) 8323 9666; Fax: (08) 8323 9600

Maggie Beer's Pheasant Farm Shop
Tel: (08) 8563 0204; Fax: (08) 8563 0763

Market 190
Tel: (08) 8323 8558; Fax: (08) 8323 7505

Nibs Restaurant
Tel: (08) 8736 3006

Reilly's Wines and Restaurant
Tel: (08) 8843 9013; Fax: (08) 8843 9013

Salopian Inn
Tel: (08) 8323 8769; Fax: (08) 8323 9311

Salters Restaurant
Tel: (08) 8564 3344; Fax: (08) 8564 3377

Siemers Indian Restaurant
Tel: (08) 8339 2235; Fax: (08) 8339 2235

Skillogalee Winery and Restaurant
Tel: (08) 8843 4311; Fax: (08) 8843 4343

St Hallett's Cafe and Bistro
Tel: (08) 8563 7000; Fax: (08) 8563 7001

Tatehams Restaurant & Guesthouse
Tel: (08) 8849 2030; Fax: (08) 8849 2260

The Hermitage Cafe and Wine Bar
Tel: (08) 8738 2122; Fax: (08) 8738 2820

The Magill Estate Restaurant
Tel: (08) 8301 5551; Fax: (08) 8301 5554

The Oxford Dining Room
Tel: (08) 8267 2652; Fax: (08) 8239 1089

The Sweet Grape
Tel: (08) 8737 2967; Fax: (08) 8737 2986

Universal Wine Bar
Tel: (08) 8232 5000; Fax: (08) 8232 5757

Vintners Bar & Grill
Tel: (08) 8564 2488; Fax: (08) 8564 2433

Woodstock Winery and Coterie
Tel: (08) 8383 0156; Fax: (08) 8383 0437

Zilm's Gourmet Cafe
Tel: (08) 8564 0003; Fax: (08) 8564 0008

Victoria

Cafe Di Stasio
Tel: (03) 9525 3999; Fax: (03) 9525 3815

Circa, The Prince
Tel: (03) 9536 1122; Fax: (03) 9536 1133

Cope-Williams Winery and Country Club
Tel: (03) 5429 5428; Fax: (03) 5429 5655

De Bortoli Winery & Restaurant
Tel: (03) 5965 2271; Fax: (03) 5965 2442

Est. Est. Est.
Tel: (03) 9682 5688; Fax: (03) 9682 5644

Ezard at Adelphi
Tel: (03) 9639 6811; Fax: (03) 9639 6822

Gennaro's Table, Villa Primavera
Tel: (03) 5989 2129; Fax: (03) 5989 2855

Kellybrook Winery Restaurant
Tel: (03) 9722 1304; Fax: (03) 9722 2092

La Baracca Trattoria
at T'Gallant
Tel: (03) 5989 6565; Fax: (03) 5989 6577

Lake House Restaurant
Tel: (03) 5348 3329; Fax: (03) 5348 3995

Lillydale International
Tel: (03) 9735 0555; Fax: (03) 9739 5692

Max's at Red Hill Estate
Tel: (03) 5989 2838; Fax: (03) 5989 2855

McWilliam's Lillydale Vineyards
Barbecue Restaurant
Tel: (03) 5964 2016; Fax: (03) 5964 3009

Milawa Epicurean Centre
Tel: (03) 5720 5500; Fax: (03) 5720 5511

Mitchelton Wine Bar Restaurant
Tel: (03) 5736 2222; Fax: (03) 5736 2266

Morning Star Estate Winery & Bistro
Tel: (03) 9787 7760; Fax: (03) 9787 7160

The Pickled Sisters Café
Tel: (02) 6033 2377; Fax: (02) 6033 2577

'The Terrace Restaurant'
at All Saints Estate
Tel: (02) 6033 1922; Fax: (02) 6033 3515

The Yarra Glen Grand Hotel
Tel: (03) 9730 1230; Fax: (03) 9730 1124

Willow Creek Vineyard Restaurant
Tel: (03) 5989 7448; Fax: (03) 5989 7584

Yering Station Wine Bar
Tel: (03) 9730 1107; Fax: (03) 9739 0135

New South Wales

Bassano Cafe
Tel: (02) 6964 4544

Cafe Crocodile at Wandin Valley Estate
Tel: (02) 4930 7317; Fax: (02) 4930 7814

Celsius Restaurtant
Tel: (02) 8214 0496; Fax: (02) 8214 0495

Craigmoor Restaurant
at Poet's Corner Winery
Tel: (02) 6373 3853; Fax: (02) 6373 3795

Darling Mills Restaurant
Tel: (02) 9660 5666; Fax: (02) 9660 8313

Elizabeth's Café at Mount Pleasant Wines
Tel: (02) 4998 7505; Fax: (02) 4998 7761

Highland Heritage Estate
Tel: (02) 6361 7381; Fax: (02) 6362 6183

Roberts at Pepper Tree Wines
Tel: (02) 4998 7539; Fax: (02) 4998 7746

Rockpool
Tel: (02) 9252 1888; Fax: (02) 9252 2421

The Cellar Restaurant
Tel: (02) 4998 7584; Fax: (02) 4998 7544

The Quarry Restaurant
Tel: (02) 6342 3650

Western Australia

Cullen Dining
Tel: (08) 9755 5277; Fax: (08) 9755 5550

Flutes Café of Brookland Valley
Tel: (08) 9755 6250; Fax: (08) 9755 6077

Fraser's Restaurant
Tel: (08) 9481 7100; Fax: (08) 9481 1319

Jackson's
Tel: (08) 9328 1177; Fax: (08) 9228 1144

Leeuwin Estate Restaurant
Tel: (08) 9757 6253; Fax: (08) 9759 0001

The Balcony Restaurant, Vasse Felix
Tel: (08) 9755 5242; Fax: (08) 9755 5425

Voyager Estate Restaurant
Tel: (08) 9757 6354; Fax: (08) 9757 6405

Tasmania

A Splash of Paris
Tel: (03) 6224 2200; Fax: (03) 6224 9635

Alexander's Restaurant
Tel: (03) 6232 3900; Fax: (03) 6224 0112

Fee and Me
Tel: (03) 6331 3195; Fax: (03) 6331 1617

Moorilla Estate Restaurant
Tel: (03) 6277 9900; Fax: (03) 6249 4093

Ninth Island Winery Restaurant:
Tel: (03) 6382 7122; Fax: (03) 6382 7225

Stillwater River Café
Tel: (03) 6331 4153; Fax: (03) 6331 2325

The Strathlynn, Strathlynn Wine Centre
Tel: (03) 6330 2388; Fax: (03) 6330 2599

The Winery Cafe, Pipers Brook
Tel: (03) 6382 7529; Fax: (03) 6382 7226

Queensland

Ballandean Estate Winery
Tel: (07) 4684 1226; Fax: (07) 4684 1288

Canungra Valley Vineyard Restaurant
Tel: (07) 5543 4011; Fax: (07) 5543 4162

Restaurant Lurleen's, Mount Cotton
Tel: (07) 3206 2999; Fax: (07) 3206 0900

Compiled by Peter Fuller & Associates

Weights and Measures

For best results when you prepare the recipes, use standard metric measures (250ml cup, 20ml tablespoon and 5ml teaspoon) unless otherwise stated.*

Follow recipe instructions carefully, use level measurements and follow the specified cooking times. The oven temperature table below is a guide only. For best accuracy, refer to your own cooker instruction book.

*In Australia, 1 tablespoon = 20ml.
In NZ, USA and UK, 1 tablespoon = 15ml.

OVEN SETTING EQUIVALENTS (TO NEAREST 10°C)			
Description	Fahrenheit	Celsius	Gas Regulo No.
Very cool	225–275	110–140	1/4–1
Cool	300–325	150–160	2–3
Moderate	350–375	180–190	4–5
Hot	400–450	200–230	6–8
Very hot	475–500	250–260	9–10

GRAMS TO OUNCES			
These are converted to the nearest round number			
GRAMS	OUNCES	GRAMS	OUNCES
25 =	1	250 =	9
50 =	2	275 =	10
75 =	3	300 =	10.5
100 =	3.5	325 =	11
125 =	4	350 =	12
150 =	5	375 =	13
175 =	6	400 =	14
200 =	7	425 =	15
225 =	8	450 =	16
1 kilogram = 1000 grams = 2lb 4oz			

Glossary

Aioli: true mayonnaise (made with egg yolk and oil) including fresh garlic.

Arborio: a risotto rice with large, plump grains.

Ballotine: meat, poultry, game or fish, boned, stuffed and rolled into a small bundle. After cooking it may be served hot or cold.

Botrytised: wine made from ripe, healthy grapes affected by the fungus *Botrytis cinerea*. Good botrytis, known as noble rot, concentrates grape sugar and acidity, adding complexity of flavour. These grapes make great sweet dessert wines.

Butternut: a winter squash, (sometimes called butternut pumpkin). An elongated pear-shape with thin, buff-coloured skin, its golden flesh is finer, paler, and less mealy then pumpkin flesh.

Chats potatoes: baby new potatoes, or small, smooth-skinned potatoes.

Ciabatta: an Italian bread; this small oval loaf is supposed to resemble a slipper in shape.

Chorizo: highly spiced sausage of Spanish origin.

Concassé: of tomatoes, skinned, deseeded and coarsely chopped.

Cotechino: a large Italian pork sausage, usually boiled and served hot with vegetables.

Dariole mould: small, bucket-shaped metal container (about 65mm high), for steaming or baking individual cakes, or puddings, or for setting gelatine or cream mixtures.

Dashi: broth made from kelp and dried bonito (a fish). Instant dashi powder mixed with boiling water may be used.

Deglaze: (déglacer) to swirl a liquid or stock with sediment left in a roasting pan or fry-pan; heat and stir with liquid to loosen the food particles.

Eschalot: shallot, (French: échalote), member of the onion family. Small, reddish-brown-skinned bulbs made up of cloves loosely joined at the base. Flesh often slightly streaked with purple. Milder and sweeter in flavour than onions.

Farce: savoury forcemeat or stuffing.

Glass noodles: very fine, wiry looking noodles made from mung bean and tapioca starch. Sold in tight, silvery white bundles labelled green bean thread vermicelli. Also called cellophane noodles. They become transparent when softened in water or deep-fried.

Haloumi: a sheep's milk cheese of Greek origin. Firm, creamy white, stretched curd cheese, matured in brine, but not as salty as feta. Can be cut into chunks and grilled and added to salads.

Hard crack: the temperature of boiling sugar solution, 150°C, when the cooled syrup will crack like glass but has not begun to colour.

Julienne: matchstick-sized strips, especially of vegetables.

Jus: juice, usually of meat. May be roasting pan juices, unthickened, or diluted with liquid (water, stock, wine) and boiled to reduce and concentrate. The pan may be deglazed with wine to pick up meat flavours, then simmered to produce jus – e.g. cabernet jus.

Kennebec potatoes: cream-skinned, white-fleshed floury potato, good for frying as chips. Suitable for baking, roasting and mashing, but not for salads.

Leaf gelatine: stiff, cellophane-like sheet gelatine. To use, cover sheets with cold water, soak for about 5 minutes to soften, then squeeze in your hands to remove excess water. Add softened sheets to hot liquid. Two sheets gelatine are equivalent to 1 teaspoon powdered gelatine.

Lentilles du Puy: deep green/blue lentils grown around Le Puy in France, renowned for their flavour.

Maldon salt: sea salt produced in Maldon, England. The particularly soft, flaky crystals may be sprinkled directly onto food or easily ground in a salt mill.

Marron: Western Australian freshwater crayfish. Also known as koonac and gilgie.

Mizuna: feathery, pretty green leaves with mild flavour, often included in salad mix.

Nam pla: Thai fish sauce made from fermented small fish or shrimps.

Nori: greenish/black dried seaweed sheet used for wrapping sushi.

Ocean trout: a member of the salmon trout family; firm, moist, orange/pink flesh with mild flavour.

Palm sugar: made from palm sap, a coarse, brown sugar with treacle-like flavour, sold in cakes.

Panna Cotta: literally 'cooked cream'. A dessert of Italian origin, creamy milk, lightly sweetened and set with gelatine.

Pecorino: Italian name given to cheeses made from sheep's milk.

Quenelle: small dumpling, usually oval, of finely minced fish, chicken or meat, poached. 'To quenelle' means to shape small ovals of soft food (e.g. mousse or avocado purée) using two dessert spoons.

Reduce: to concentrate a liquid or stock by simmering or boiling.

Rocket: (French: roquette, Italian cress), a tasty salad green, mildly spicy when leaves are young and pale green, more peppery in darker, mature leaves. Enlivens salads.

Roma tomatoes: a variety of long, egg-shaped or plum tomato with firm flesh.

Sichuan (Szechwan) peppercorns: dried, reddish-brown berries of a type of ash tree. Also called anise-pepper, Chinese pepper. Flavour sharp and mildly peppery.

Seal or sear: to brown or colour, or to set the surface of meat, usually a preliminary step using high heat and brief cooking in a hot pan or oven.

Spanish onion: creamy-yellow-skinned onion variety, sweeter and less pungent than white or brown-skinned onions.

Sweat: to cook food (usually vegetables) slowly with a little butter or oil in a pan (with lid on) without colouring, until the food exudes juices. A preliminary step for soup-making and stewing.

Tagliolini: narrow ribbon noodles, finer than tagliatelle or fettuccine.

Tahini: sesame paste.

Udon noodles: large, white Japanese noodles.

Verjuice (verjus): acid juice of unripe grapes, less sharp in flavour than lemon juice or vinegar; may be used in place of either in vinaigrette. Refrigerate after opening.

Vialone nano: a risotto rice. This has a smaller grain than arborio rice and a little more resistance to the bite when cooked.

Vietnamese mint: long, thin mint leaves with strong flavour.

Yabby: a freshwater crayfish, smaller than a marron.

Zatar: (zathar) a sour aromatic Middle Eastern seasoning; a mixture of thyme and sumac.

Recipe Index

Trade inquiries to:
Bookwise International Pty Ltd
174 Cormack Rd, Wingfield, SA 5013
Phone: 08 0268 8222
Fax: 08 0268 8704
Email: orders@bookwise.com.au

First published by Chanel Publishers Ltd, 2001
© Photography: Ian Baker
© Text: Chanel Publishers Ltd
© Recipes: Remain with the contributing restaurants

Publisher: Cliff Josephs
Publishing manager: Barbara Nielsen
Photographer: Ian Baker
Text writer: Sally Marden
Editorial research: Peter Fuller & Associates
Editorial assistant: William Fuller
Recipe editing and research: Elisabeth Pedersen
Design: Sally Hollis McLeod, Moscow Design
Printed by: Midas Printing (Asia) Ltd.

ISBN: 0-958208-44-1